Past Poets – Future Voices

2010 Poetry Competition for 11-18 year-olds

The Midlands & South Yorkshire

Edited by Allison Jones

First published in Great Britain in 2010 by

Remus House
Coltsfoot Drive
Peterborough
PE2 9JX
Telephone: 01733 890066
Website: www.youngwriters.co.uk

All Rights Reserved
Book Design by Ali Smith & Tim Christian
© Copyright Contributors 2010
SB ISBN 978-0-85739-188-9

Foreword

Young Writers was established in order to promote creativity and a love of reading and writing in children and young adults. We believe that by offering them a chance to see their own work in print, their confidence will grow and they will be encouraged to become the poets of tomorrow.

Our latest competition 'Past Poets - Future Voices' was specifically designed as a showcase for secondary school pupils, giving them a platform with which to express their ideas, aspirations and passions. In order to expand their skills, entrants were encouraged to use different forms, styles and techniques.

Selecting the poems for publication was a difficult yet rewarding task and we are proud to present the resulting anthology. We hope you agree that this collection is an excellent insight into the voices of the future.

Contents

Caludon Castle School, Wyken
Alisha Butle (12) 1
Safina Siddiqui (14) 3
Danielle Beckett (12) 4
Chloe Van Der Merwe (11) 5
Lewis Beavis (12) 5
Vicky Porter (13) 6
Abi Davies (12) 6
Abi Wells (12) 7
Lydia Herron (14) 8
Callum Price (12) 9

Castle Vale School & Performing Arts College, Birmingham
Eloise Whittingham (11) 9
Antonia Yvonne Sloan (13) 10
Samantha Woods (13) 11
Bradley Broadmore (11) 12
Sinead Egan (13) 13
Heitienne Guimaraes (12) 14
Kara Coles (13) 15
Kellie Hendrickson (13) 15
Chance Harris (13) 16
Kelsey Evans (12) 16
Claire Oldbury (12) 17
Bradley Smith (13) 17
Ryan Musson (13) 18
Shazaib Khukhar (14) 19
Chloe Blythe (12) 19
Philip Cornish (12) 20
Emily Currah (13) 20

Coventry Muslim School, Coventry
Naailah Dawood (12) 21
Aisha Ayub (12) 22
Maryam Shahid (12) 22
Malisa Miah (12) 23
Humera Khalifa (11) 23
Sulekha Hassan Hussein (13) 24
Jemila Kamila Saifi (12) 24
Iqra Nowal (12) 25
Hafsa Khan (14) 25

Danum School Technology College, Doncaster
Katie Marshall (16) 27
Karina Iwaszkiewicz (15) 27
Charlotte Utting (13) 28
Sophie Croxall (12) 28
Megan Cooper (13) 29
Emily Johnsen (12) 31
Tariro Chitiyo (13) 31
Kelsey Douthwaite (12) 32
Tayana Howell (14) 32
Kelsey Courtney (13) 33
Marie Gibb (12) 33
Rebecca Bosworth (12) 34
Brooke Turner
& Emma Hartshorne (13) 34
Gabriel Carr (11) 35

Ellesmere College (Secondary Special School), Leicester
Kyle Kirkland (14) 35
Uzair Suleman (13) 36

Fir Vale Secondary School, Sheffield
Adeela Ahmed (11) 36
Htet Htet Khaing Win (13) 37
Nagina Shahzadi (11) 37
Farrah Din (12) 38

Humphrey Perkins High School, Barrow Upon Soar
Ashly Millward (13) 38
Jake Gant (13) 39

Emma Haynes (13) 41
Josiah Williamson (13) 41
Daniel Hart (13) 42
Megan Barston (13) 43
George Mitchell (13) 44
Emily Fox (13) 45
Renaise Carter (13) 46
Connor Higgins (13) 47
Katie Marie Westmacott (13) 48
Kyle Archer (13) 49
Siân Lloyd-McLear (13) 50
Heidi Mumford (13) 51
Amy Walker (12) 52
Harry Smith (13) 53
Joshua Gregory (13) 54
Hannah Brooks (13) 55
Elizabeth Wells (13) 56
Katie Macdonald (13) 57
Richard Palmer (13) 58
Nathan Munden (13) 59
Jake Samardzija (13) 60
Beth Rennocks (13) 61
Hannah Greatrex (13) 62
Sam Johnson (13) 63
Hannah Hickinbotham (13) 64
Nathan Preston (13) 65
Megan Hunter (12) 66
Sam Mottram (13) 67
Emily Bacon (12) 68
Aiden McWeeney (13) 69
Joe Darling (13) 70
Owen Chamberlain (12) 71
James Harman-Thomas (13) 72
Robert Shuttlewood (13) 73
Joseph Myko (12) 74
Harvey Gaunt (13) 75
Alice Lees (13) 76
Paige Hewes (13) 77
Max Ratcliffe (13) 78
Christian Warren (13) 79
Jamie Stenning (13) 80
Samantha Vesty (13) 81
Sophie Nelson (13) 82
George Thompson (13) 83

James Brindley School, Birmingham
Tatiana Lelo (17) 84
Ebony Danielle Melrose (17) 85

Leicester High School for Girls, Leicester
Rebecca Millar (16) 87
Simran Roshan (10) 87
Hannah Bristow (17) 89
Sania Akhtar-Hassan (10) 89
Phoebe Love (11) 90
Aditi Pant (11) 90
Anya Agnihotri (11) 91
Georgie Parker (11) 92
Verity Howell (11) 92

Lincoln Minster School, Lincoln
Henry Bennison (16) 93

Newport Girls' High School, Newport
Beth Higgins (14) 94
Tabitha Heeley (14) 95
Jenny Smith (13) 96
Emma Higgins (14) 97
Naomi Gulliver (14) 98
Ellie Bryan (14) 99
Jen Clarke (14) 100
Lucie Price (14) 101
Dimple Mistry (14) 102
Kayleigh Woodhouse (14) 103

Ninestiles School, Acocks Green
Christian Luke Da'Costa (16) 104
Andrew Parry (16) 105

Northampton College, Northampton
Nicolette Hibbert (18) 106

St George's Academy, Sleaford
Jo Pilkington (14) 107
Charlie Strachan (13) 108
Chloe Blades (14) 109

St Thomas Aquinas Catholic School, Kings Norton
Liam Conroy (14) 109
Danea Campbell (14) 110
Hannah Doyle (14) 111
Kavan Green (13) 112
Alice McIntosh (14) 113
Daniel Moore (14) 114
Rebecca Dunbar (14) 114
Hannah Sweeney (14) 115
Jordan Pinnock-Miller (14) 115
Charmaine Espinoza (14) 116
John Raven (14) 116
Cleopatra Madziwa (13) 117
Declan Reville (14) 117
Matthew Georgiou (14) 118
Tre'Rail Peters (13) 118
Luke Kiely (14) 119
Courtney Burley (13) 119
Luke Farrell (14) 120
Claire Walsh (14) 120
Molly McDonald (13) 121
Jodie Carey (14) 121
Josh Gannon (14) 122
Joel Healy (14) 122
Ellen Herbert (13) 123
Paige Ridley (14) 123
Liam Connolly (14) 124
Adam McKinley (14) 124
Hafsa Rehman (13) 125

Sheffield High School, Sheffield
Megan Cave &
Aliji Ntima Garvis (12) 125
Jennyfer Reid (13) 127
Maddy Darling (12) 127
Tayla Shelley (14) 129
Rhea Jain (12) 129
Francesca Diiasio (13) 131
Ellie Needham (13) 131
Shani Gill (12) 133
Lois Rands (13) 133
Natalia Hackett (13) 135
Rachel Bricklebank (13) 135
Olivia Noble (13) 137
Lynne Shackshaft (13) 137
Alice Strong (13) 139
Sarah Felicity Talbot (13) 139
Olivia Roberts (13) 140
Elizabeth Rawson (13) 141
Amadora Frogson (13) 142
Siobhan Prentice (13) 143
Felicia Bi (12) 144
Nadeen Jawad (12) 145
Daniz Mobayen (13) 146
Rebecca Higgins (12) 147
Sophia Livoti (13) 148
Grace Shurmer (13) 149
Humera Riaz (13) 150
Abbie Danielle Linell (13) 151
Tegan Caddy (13) 152
Olivia Beavers (13) 153
Charlotte Farrugia (13) 154
Wankumbu Chisala (13) 155
Kazna Asker (13) 156
Molly Norman &
Melissa White (13) 157
Juliet Armstrong (13) 158
Trishna Kurian (12) 158
Nikita Azeem (13) 159
Frances Anderson (12) 159
Holly West (12) 160
Olivia Pryor (13) 160
Sarah Lee-Liggett (12) 161
Emma Nicole Spencer (13) 161
Tanvi Acharya (13) 162
Sophie Peckett (12) 162
Roshni Timms (13) 163
Georgia Tracey &
Sarah Throssell (11) 163

Lara Conboy (13) 164
Sarah Anne Myers (13) 164
Jessica Askham (12) 165
Eleanor Hyde (11) 166

Sir Graham Balfour School, Stafford

Jonty Farmer (12) 166
Charlotte Hall (13) 167
Kiera Robinson (13) 168
Erin Softley (13) 169
Katie Nichol (13) 170
Rob Bowyer (13) 171
Charlotte Forrester (13) 172
Tamsin Tolfree (12) 173
Oliver McCoy (13) 174
Sarina Patel (13) 175
Stephanie Essery (13) 176
Kayleigh Steel (13) 177
Ella Platt 178
Toby Hollinshead (13) 179
Poppy Fletcher (13) 180
Oliver Dracup-Nicholls (13) 180
Valentina Calleja (13) 181
Emma Forrester (13) 181
Jemma Barlow (13) 182
Flo Peczek (13) 182

Sir Henry Cooper School, Hull

Ashley Powley (12) 183
Cydnee Jones (11) 184
Molly Toker (11) 184
Ellie Wetherell (12) 185
Kane Sutherby (12) 185
Declan Pidd (12) 186
Layla Alison (11) 187
Danielle Johnson (12) 187
James Hall (12) 188

Solihull School, Solihull

Jacob Seickell (14) 188
Luke Carr (14) 189
Grace Lodge (13) 191

Amy Hughes (15) 193
Oscar Street (15) 193
Charlotte Beesley (14) 194
Lottie Wilson (14) 195
Katherine Bridges (14) 195
Matthew Tyler (14) 196
Elizabeth Ready (14) 196
Callum Fisher (14) 197
Taimoor Rashid (14) 197
Matthew Bottomley (14) 198

The Northicote School, Wolverhampton

Emily Riley (11) 198
Lydia Dungey (15) 199
Lauren Smith 199
Louise Weaver (15) 201
Elizabeth Elliot 201
Shaneaqua Edwards (13) 202
Hayley Samuels (12) 202
Tor Bennett Williams (11) 203
Paige Woods (15) 203
Sam Bentham (15) 204
Charlotte Skidmore (14) 204
Luke Chagger (12) 205
Megan Gallagher 205
Amy Evans (12) 205
Samantha Nightingale (15) 206

The Orchard Centre (PRU), Wolverhampton

Rhiannon Thorpe (16) 206
Lewis Turton (14) 207
Julia Scheyer (14) 208
Mariah Antill (15) 209
Victoria Louise Shaw (13) 210
Rebecca Goodhead (14) 210
Joe Goldsmith (12) 211
Edward Shore (12) 211
Jordan Lloyd (13) 212
Chelsea Williams (13) 212
Callum Derek Andrews (14) 213
Glyn Anthony Cieron Smith (13) 214
Seranne Behenna (13) 214

Beth Nangle (14) 215
Jasmine Ross (14) 215
Cameron Nock (15) 216

Wickersley School & Sports College, Wickersley

Shannon Jones &
Megan Lockwood (14) 216
Ben Higgins (14) 217
Shirley Ngan (12) 219
Molly Burtoft (13) 219
Joe Oxspring (12) 220
Jemma Poole, Devon Round (14)
& Nicole Turtle (13) 221
Matthew Boyce-Boardman (14)
& Oliver King (13) 222
Anya Gill (12) 222
Emilia Shillito (11) 223
Jemma Daisy Heathcoate (12) 224
Lauren Wainwright (13) 225
Alana Jackson
& Chanelle Clarke (13) 226
Christian Hague (12) 226
Georgina Gunn, Hollie Sheppard
& Courtney Sutton (14) 227
Lauren Carr (11) 227
Nicole Cooper
& Eleanor Dovey (12) 228
Sophie Gibson (13) 228
Chloe Wilkinson (12) 229
Owen King (12) 229
Zak Anthony Bailey (13) 230
Abigail Adams
& Hannah Horton (12) 230
Meghan Webb (12) 231
Oliver Blake & Alex Stronach (12) ... 231
Michael Taylor (11) 232
Aisha Mahmood (11) 232

William Bradford Community College, Earl Shilton

Luke Parkes (15) 233
Ryan Oswald (14) 234
Elysia Newton (14) 235
Jasmin Copson (15) 236
Chelsea King (15) 236
Amy Armitage (15) 237
Conor Salmon (14) 237
Ben Glew (14) 238
Jonnie Skinner (14) 238
Lewis Wright (15) 239
Eve Elizabeth Moth (15) 239
Keiran Gibbs (15) 240
Katie Short (14) 241
Bethany Keenan (15) 241
Shannon Hewitt (15) 242
Kellie-Anne Pakes (15) 242
Faye Whittley (15) 243
Stephen Orton
& Zack Taylor (15) 243
Matthew Ceeney (14) 244

The Poems

Mum

For someone as special as you
Words are hard to find . . .
But caring, kind and thoughtful
Are just three that come to mind

More and more caring she gets
My mum that's what she stands for
Happy and pleased to be with me
Making me feel lucky

She is a good person
You can see it in her eyes
Knows what's best for me all the time
Whether it's at school or at home

She is there for me all the time
At home or even at school sometimes
And when I need a shoulder to cry on
I know she's there for me

My mum is trustworthy, she never lives
She tells me the truth even if she knows I might cry
But she knows that when I eventually
Find out the truth it will hurt even more now.

My mum is supportive all the time
She supports my schoolwork and my homework
She helps me study for tests
Even when most of the times
She doesn't know what it's about.

My mum is loving more than you can imagine
Every day from when I wake up
Till I got to bed she never forgets
To tell me that she loves me.

Alisha Butle (12)
Caludon Castle School, Wyken

The Stage

Some of us linger around the dressing room
Make-up and props at the ready
Frantic others rush around at last minute
Is that the final call already?

We listen carefully for our names to be called
To pay attention, we stretch our ears
One last warm up before we're up on stage
Get ready for the smiles and tears.

The curtains rise, bit by bit
Our nerves must disappear
And so we begin tonight's performance
As we listen to the audience cheer.

Our minds are concentrating hard
For two hours of the night
But we still have fun and never disappoint
As we're standing in the spotlight.

Sometimes the lights tend to burn our eyes
So careful not to look up
As the curtains come down for the interval
We run for our coffee cup.

Too soon is our two minute call
But we're excited nevertheless
Click our fingers and we're back in role
It's like we're being possessed.

Back on stage it's the dramatic scene
So we put our smiles away
Costumes changed, a new backdrop
As if it's another day.

The next scene arrives, it's the cheerful one
Everyone's happy, everything's bliss
Just before the finale, the audience cheer
But there's one thing people seem to miss.

A character isn't our real selves
Just a person we portray
Nothing like the way we are

In what we do or what we say.

Sometimes the stage is too real in life
With people acting different all the time
One minute all sweet and innocent
The next they're crossing the line.

Acting different just to impress one another
May as well be a world contest
Shocks me how two-sided some can be
It's like they're being possessed.

Some people have made me wonder
Who on earth is that I see?
Same face, same looks, but empty eyes
Staring straight back at me.

Do you honestly think they have a clue
Who they really are inside
Or have their souls been forgotten on stage
Their real lives left behind?

End of the show, so take a bow
The performance has come to an end
But one day I hope you'll realise
A character on stage is only pretend.

Safina Siddiqui (14)
Caludon Castle School, Wyken

The Girl With The Red Eyes

The full moon
A source of eerie light
Whistles of red, black and white
Through the trees at blinding speed
The girl with the red eyes halts to feed.

The eyes sparkling
Skin, silver in the moonlight
Red hair like flames burning your frail human eyes
Lips, soft, red, rose petals
A perfect statue is the girl with the red eyes.

A cat's agility
Pouncing at a limp deer
Draining its blood and fear
Eyes glowing with triumph
Her gleaming white teeth
Set in a dark smile
The girl with the red eyes.

Danger! Danger!
Humans around
The girl up a tree with no sound
Eyes glinting with a weak red light
A human in shock as he sees
The girl with the red eyes
Renesmee ...

Danielle Beckett (12)
Caludon Castle School, Wyken

Edward

His large masculine body
Pearl-white and ice-cold
As smooth as marble
As hard as rock
His skin, glistening
In the dim-lit meadow.
He was the most beautiful thing there
Shadowing all the flowers and moss-embellished tree trunks
He was an angel
From a fairy tale
He definitely wasn't real.
His eyes
A golden butterscotch
Almost making me dizzy.
I stumbled closer, reaching my arms out
His fragrance was impossible to describe
But just one sniff sent my mind craving for more.
I felt myself running to his touch . . .
And then the book snapped shut.

Chloe Van Der Merwe (11)
Caludon Castle School, Wyken

George

George was very slow
He didn't know where to go
He tried his best to pass his test
But had to stop to have a rest.

He never listened when he was at school
Which made him feel like a very old fool.

George had the stamina
To become the examiner
He had the most extreme power
But couldn't stay awake more than an hour.

Lewis Beavis (12)
Caludon Castle School, Wyken

He Has Nothing

He was sitting in the corner
Of the cold, damp street
Weather was the opposite to a sauna
And he had no food and nothing to eat
His clothes were old and worn out
With only one shoe
And on his face a big pout
His things were the opposite to new.
Everyone walking past
Not caring at all
How does he last
With no family to call?
I don't understand how he can cope
Just sitting there day after day
I give him lots of faith and hope
Which every night I pray.
Bless this man with nothing at all
To help him is my plan, in my arms he can fall.

Vicky Porter (13)
Caludon Castle School, Wyken

Oceans

Oceans and your glorious waves,
Floating gracefully across the seabed,
Swishing away all of your mysteries,
People have searched for centuries to discover your wonders
And uncover your secrets,
You give us clues about what we seek,
And help us to move further
But it is not always trusted by you and your salty waves,
As we seep into your icy kingdom
You have some things to say
Beware these dreaded waves!
As we may not be as gentle as you say . . .

Abi Davies (12)
Caludon Castle School, Wyken

Holiday

The sparkly blue sea
Dances up the beach
I feel free
Biting into a cold, juicy peach.

Sunglasses resting on head
Cold cocktail in hand
Lying on a sunbed
Kids playing in the sand.

Sitting at the edge
Feet dangling in the cool pool
The smell of a potato wedge
Coming from the food stall.

Clothes flying all over the place
The rush of going home packing
Too much suncream - what a waste
Finally overcoming my fright of flying.

Abi Wells (12)
Caludon Castle School, Wyken

When My War Is Over

When my war is over
Homeward bound I'll be
I'm not the boy who went to war
A battered man they will see.

We joined up for adventure
Answering Kitchener's call
Brothers in arms fighting side by side
I will remember them all.

When my war is over
And this mud-soaked trench is home no more
How much we will welcome the silence
What has this sacrifice been for?

We are the lucky ones, who have survived
Let there be no other war
I'm not sure if I can tell them
Of the horrors that I saw.

Lydia Herron (14)
Caludon Castle School, Wyken

My Holiday - Sonnet

The soft warm sand tickles my tiny toes
The waves roar past the windy hours of the day
The surfers cautiously slide all day long
Babies crying because they're getting wet.

I'm playing volleyball with all my friends
I eat an ice cream with a chocolate Flake
I talk to my family all day long
I swim all the way to the furthest buoy.

The heat from the sun blazes at my neck
All of my family laugh at a joke
The lifeguard says to me, 'Hi Son, how are you?'
The clouds come overhead so bye-bye.

I have got to go so ta-ta, bye-bye
I leave the hotel with a great big sigh.

Callum Price (12)
Caludon Castle School, Wyken

Almost Gone For Good

Your presence is a mystery
You're the sly guy of the 'hood'
Your home has got a history
But it's almost gone for good.
Every step you take is a danger
For what if the ice should break?
Because every polar bear that stood
Has almost gone for good.
You live in an ice-filled habitat
And when I hear your feet go,
Rat-a-tat-tat
The shooting of the hunters' guns
I know that every polar bear runs
When I hear a thud
I know that one polar bear is gone for good.

Eloise Whittingham (11)
Castle Vale School & Performing Arts College, Birmingham

The End

Desolate, lost and all alone
This used to be a place people called home
Simply left adrift in space
The extinction of the human race.
A beautiful planet of green and blue
It's a shame that it happened to a planet so new
The moon set high up in the sky
The mountains so tall make you want to fly
All was lost to a war of time
To wreck such a beautiful planet
With war, famine and poverty was a crime.

Now the war is ended, all dead and gone
None of its inhabitants survived . . . not even one
The planet was destined to be famous and great
But it became cursed with tragic fate
What they achieved will live on forever
They will be remembered always and forgotten never.

But at least without them on the planet
Polluting, preventing it from being nourished
Now the planet will grow to its full extent and flourish
Lives were lost in an unnecessary cause
They'd have realised their mistake if only they had taken a short pause
What happened here will be buried in the past
All the bad memories; out they have been cast
The grass once green but now dead because of the strife
The wind does not blow through the trees to give the feeling of life
The ash hangs high in the cloud like a blanket of darkness
They destroyed this planet they wanted to harness
A sea of flowers still and silent
They grew from the blood spilled when they were being violent
To lose this planet and its worth, now all will be renewed with its rebirth
For in the future, this planet will be called Earth.

Antonia Yvonne Sloan (13)
Castle Vale School & Performing Arts College, Birmingham

My Male Inspiration

I feel safe when you are with me
If trouble calls you're always there
I feel your constant protection
Any time, any place, anywhere.

From the day that I was born
You've been right by my side
We shared hugs and laughs and teardrops
You're my inspiration and my guide.

Growing up we shared such memories
Taken lots of photos too
Looking back I've found my favourite ones
Are the ones of me and you.

From our garden to the school playground
A scary place for me to be
I needed love and reassurance
That only you could give to me.

We had to cope with sudden changes
We never knew would come our way
It got too hard to be as truthful
Hiding feelings we couldn't say.

As the future comes to find us
We will start to drift apart
Pictures fade, memories forgotten
But love never leaves the heart.

You'll think this about my dad
And how much we love each other
I shall now reveal my truest hero
Is actually my brother.

Samantha Woods (13)
Castle Vale School & Performing Arts College, Birmingham

Aliens

Aliens came home last Monday night
They gave me quite a fright
One was called Blob and the other Slob
And they went, 'Dib, dib, dob, dob!'
They said they wanted food
But I wasn't in the mood
I hit them with a chair
But they went up the stair

I looked for them high and low
Then I saw my dog Bo
He was acting really weird
Then I saw Slob wearing a fake beard
I ripped it off his face
I forgot to tie my lace
I tripped over my brother's truck
I wasn't having much luck.

I finally got out
But it was 1 o'clock about
I calmed down drinking a cup of tea
But then I looked at the tree
The aliens were still here,
'Oh no, oh dear, oh dear!'

I thought I was seeing things
Until they took off a bird's wing,
'Shoo, you pest,' I said out loud
They went away and I was proud
But look at all this mess
I'll blame it on my cat Jess.

Bradley Broadmore (11)
Castle Vale School & Performing Arts College, Birmingham

Moon's Curse

It's tormenting me day by day
Week by week, year by year
I can't take it anymore
My heart is crumbling away, like the rocks of an eroding volcano
The hot burning lava burns my organs and insides
All I can do is sit and suffer
As the full moon floats in the night sky, it watches my every move
It sparkles onto the lake
The reflection shimmers and shines across the valley
The pain becomes more intense
I feel my spine gradually curving into an arch
I try to force my back to stop but it's not working
My face grows long and thin
I can smell everything around me
But all the colours fade to black and white
My arms and legs ship shape
So I can no longer stand on two legs but four paws
The pain stops
I no longer feel weak
I feel rage
There is so much fury in me
I can feel my blood starting to boil and bubble
I look up at my beloved and sing along
I sing with my brothers and sisters
We sing to the curse of the moon.

Sinead Egan (13)
Castle Vale School & Performing Arts College, Birmingham

Why Am I Here?

A dark shroud that covered my birth
I'm in a new home on a planet called Earth
Why am I here in this barbaric wasteland
Filled with horrible creatures who walk in the sand?
But then I see it, my passion burns like seven suns

We can't be but one star, we can't be
But why, why must I suffer in pain?
My heart's just beating like I've been hit by a train.

But love is a game that we all play
So keep on your toes, it will be OK
It's like at school when I was a little boy
I had my favourite toy
But a big guy took away my pride
I was intimidated, low-rated, took a dictionary and cried.

Definition of a bully: an attention-seeking beast
On the little ones; goes for the weak
Lives in a world of fantasy
He quotes, 'No one is stronger than me'
He doesn't care what he's doing to you
But the pain and the hurt that he puts you through
He just takes your money and kills your pride
You will get so scared that you'll run and hide.

Heitienne Guimaraes (12)
Castle Vale School & Performing Arts College, Birmingham

The End Of Time!

At the end of time
This poem may not rhyme
What will it be like?

Will there be wars
Or laws?
Or maybe we'll be able to fly
In the big blue sky?
It would be good if people were green
And the Earth was clean!

Will there be flying cars too
Travelling to Mars?
Food in imaginary tins?
Fish with no fins?

Will colours be bright?
Will it still be daylight?
So many questions . . . not many answers.

We should live forever
And ever
But then it would not be the end of time.

Kara Coles (13)
Castle Vale School & Performing Arts College, Birmingham

George

I miss the way you used to stare
I miss the way you brush your hair
I miss your eyes, I miss your face
Although I know you're in a better place.

I just think back on all the times
The day I got you, the day you were mine
I still see and hear and smell you now
But I'll remember you are looking down.

Kellie Hendrickson (13)
Castle Vale School & Performing Arts College, Birmingham

Fame And Fortune

Skin of dog, both male and grey
A baby born on the Sabbath day
A tail of ginger cat
The limp wings of a flightless bat
Saturn's ring
And a hornet's sting

Stir it with a reaper's scythe
A weapon of an endless life

A heavenly cloud
And Hell's dark shroud
Drop in a coin of great wealth
And wish me fortune and good health
Drop in a painting of van Gogh
And fame and fortune I shall know

Drop in a symbolic raven's wing
And a widow's engagement ring
Tame, tame the ravenous flame
And give me health, wealth and fame.

Chance Harris (13)
Castle Vale School & Performing Arts College, Birmingham

My Sister

My sister can never tell the time
She takes out all of my stuff
I say to her, 'Hey, that's mine!'
She always gets what she wants
I only get what I want once

She always has to cry
On the settee she has to cry
At the end of the day
In my bed I lay
But I will always lover her.

Kelsey Evans (12)
Castle Vale School & Performing Arts College, Birmingham

Seasons

The Earth has different seasons
These seasons are wonderful things
The wind comes in winter
The snow is even better
It's dry in spring
It's the main Easter thing
But rains in autumn
Different coloured trees lined in column
In summer it's sunny
When the bees produce their honey

People always ask
Why the seasons pass
And the answer to that
The Earth is tilted not flat
This is why we get hot while having fun
When we are furthest away from the sun
The winter has just begun.

Claire Oldbury (12)
Castle Vale School & Performing Arts College, Birmingham

The Winning Goal!

Take the ball to the net
And put the opposition's defence under threat.
After the game is won
The parties have already begun.
The losers leave their seats
With their minds full of heat.
The loser's manager gets spoken to now
On what went wrong and how.
Still the celebration stays
And puts the opposition at bay.
Leaving with their heads held low
Losing that game, what a blow!

Bradley Smith (13)
Castle Vale School & Performing Arts College, Birmingham

Decisions

Halfway through Year 8 I moved schools
There were lots of changes and lots of new rules
But the line had been drawn
I had more brains than brawn.

At the old place all I could have were friends
No potential, no chances, nearly driven to the ends
I made a change and chose an education over social life
So in the future I can provide for my kids and wife.

I'm nearing Year 10, I've made my choices
Finishing my Btec, no time for rejoices
I hope in the future a good employer will hear my voice
So I can drive round in a Rolls Royce.

The message I'm trying to send out here
Is that school is not all about friends and cheer
If you want to do well, you must put in the work
Cos in a dead end job you'll look like a berk.

Ryan Musson (13)
Castle Vale School & Performing Arts College, Birmingham

A Pet Is For Life

A pet is for life or so they say
It doesn't just last for Christmas Day
A little pup has feelings too
It will always rely on you.

Treat your animal with respect
So give them the love that they expect
They will love you in return
And obedience they will learn.

As they grow older their needs will change
Longer walks you must arrange
A dog for life is a commitment
It is a very important event.
So think before you have a pet
Are you ready for this commitment yet?

Shazaib Khukhar (14)
Castle Vale School & Performing Arts College, Birmingham

Jess

I love you Jess
You're definitely not a mess
I've watched you grow every day
Let's give you a big hooray
You drive me mad
Please don't act bad
It's not your fault you're sad.

I love you, yes I do
Me and you
Forever
You like the feel of leather
Your friend is called Heather
It's not your fault you know rhymes
But now you know, please don't mime.

Chloe Blythe (12)
Castle Vale School & Performing Arts College, Birmingham

Peace

I'd rather have peace than war
I'd rather there be no conflict
Though
I'd rather fight aliens than humans
I'd rather fight for my country than to watch it die
I'd rather lay down my weapon than to use it
I'd rather say 'no' to war rather than yes
As
I'd rather say 'yes' to peace rather than no
I'd rather there be no conflict
I'd rather not fight than to fight
I'd rather say, 'Peace! than that, 'Fight!'
I'd rather there be no conflict . . .
I'd rather have peace . . . than war.

Philip Cornish (12)
Castle Vale School & Performing Arts College, Birmingham

A Sister

A sister is a friend
A sister is an enemy
It is a relationship that will never end
They always argue and fight
Then they make up
But try never to bite
You share your secrets and your dreams
You share the good and the bad
It isn't as it always seems
To laugh at each other
And people they know
Mostly they don't bother
They hope to always be together
And be friends forever.

Emily Currah (13)
Castle Vale School & Performing Arts College, Birmingham

Why?

Why do they do this?
They spit and they hiss.

They are horrible and cruel
They make us look like fools.

Why do they do this?
They spit and they hiss.

They call us terrorists
They call us extremists.

They say, 'Go back to your country.'
But this is where I belong
I haven't done anything wrong.

Why do they do this?
They spit and they hiss.

They mock and they swear
They laugh and they stare
They don't really care.

They think we don't understand
They think we're from another land.

Why do they do this?
They spit and they hiss.

They think I'm scared
But I've never really cared.

I'm here standing proud
But I've never said it aloud.

I am a Muslim!

Naailah Dawood (12)
Coventry Muslim School, Coventry

I Can See . . .

I can hear birds tweeting in sweet tune,
I can see caterpillars hanging from trees, curled in cocoons.

I can see,
I can hear,
Nature's beauty.

I can hear the gentle breeze,
I can see the golden autumn leaves.

I can see,
I can hear,
Nature's beauty.

I can hear the splish-sploshing of a lake,
I can see that nature's awake.

I can see,
I can hear,
Nature's beauty.

I can hear the buzzing of the bees,
I can see the waves of the trees.

I can see,
I can hear,
Nature's beauty.

Aisha Ayub (12)
Coventry Muslim School, Coventry

A Monday Morning

It was the first and the best
A morning on a Monday
It was fresh and clean
The smells, like bluebells and fresh grass
When the sky opens one eye and gives a wink
And the morning is as clean as water
It was the best and the first, a Monday morning!

Maryam Shahid (12)
Coventry Muslim School, Coventry

Drugs, Alcohol, Smoking

Drugs are for thugs
Smoking is for mugs
Why do they do it?
They know it's bad for your health
It takes most of your wealth.

Drugs are for thugs
Smoking is for mugs
Alcohol destroys families and lives
All these substances involve dangerous weapons such as knives
How can they do it?

Drugs are for thugs
Smoking is for mugs
People say smoking weakens stress
This is not for the best
Stop! This is ruining the world, just confess.

Drugs are for thugs
Smoking is for mugs
Just stop it right now!
This is just influencing the younger generation
How can they? How?

Malisa Miah (12)
Coventry Muslim School, Coventry

In My Happiness

In my happiness I feel the bright colours of the rainbow shining on me
In my happiness there is no unhappiness
In my happiness being scared doesn't exist
In my happiness everything makes sense
In my happiness I feel peace in my heart
In my happiness the sad times have floated like the wind, calm and gentle
In my happiness I feel ready to take on anything.

Humera Khalifa (11)
Coventry Muslim School, Coventry

Death Of Love

Water pouring down my face as if it was rain
Knowing that I have made the biggest mistake I have ever made
Love isn't what you expected when it turns out bad
They might break your heart or die when it's time
Washing the blood from my hands and face
Knowing that my heart turned black and hard as a stone
And every piece is falling from my bones
Always watch out for the one you love
As they might die and grow the wings of a dove
Blood and tears flowing with the water
And now my heart has been ripped apart
Right after I murdered the one I love.

Sulekha Hassan Hussein (13)
Coventry Muslim School, Coventry

Chocolate, Chocolate, Chocolate

Chocolates are sweet
And tasty to eat
They come in different sizes
I'd love to win as prizes
Dark chocolate is nice
But white chocolates are better
Eat too much and you'll get fatter
Overall chocolates are the best
Better than the rest.

Jemila Kamila Saifi (12)
Coventry Muslim School, Coventry

Friends

Weekend is the time to have your friends around
Playing together and making sound
Telling secrets, having fun, watching the view of the sun
Sharing jokes and wishing for magic cloaks
Which make you disappear and take you anywhere
Eating ice cream and watching a movie which makes you scream
Talking about the latest things, which makes your tummy fill with springs
Going into town so don't feel down
Coming back home and saying goodbye to your friends
So let's turn off the light and say goodnight.

Iqra Nowal (12)
Coventry Muslim School, Coventry

I've Lost You

All this time I didn't know
All this pain that you went through
All the things that I said to you
But now it's too late
Because I lost you.

Hafsa Khan (14)
Coventry Muslim School, Coventry

Broken Symmetry

Confusion is the rubric
Of solitude
Evading into all places
Where I am fully alone

There is no reflection
Where we become caught
Between each other
Out of touch and out of time

Welcoming you in
Out of the heat

The friction between our minds fades
We surrender effortlessly
Senseless, we strive for equilibrium
The boundaries are breached
We creep like shadows
Seeking lower ground

I slip through the cracks into your world
Running over the surface of you
Seeking solidarity
Level ground where we are safe
Cold like the sky
All the confused pieces of me
We drift through the space between thoughts
Through the emptiness between us

Lower than ground
We find our place
Absolution we seek to reach
Drifting with the tide and
Rising with the waves
But the lifelines never meet

Failing to find a sense of liberty
Running up the walls
Bleeding cold stone
Defiantly I climb
Like ivy
My tendrils reaching
Into the darkest corners of your mind
Hold still
Suspended.

A kind of duality
Within our limits
Blurring together
Seek to find another meaning
Freeze the pendulum
The mirror hanging in the balance
Trace your fingers along the glass
Fragile like you

Spontaneously
We break.

Katie Marshall (16)
Danum School Technology College, Doncaster

Rain

I will never change myself for anyone
I will not wear smiling masks on a crying face
I will not stick the fake tears on my smile
I will not change someone's stones under their feet into pollution
I will not stab myself with a dagger and pretend it doesn't hurt me
I will not turn back for even a step, waiting for someone to catch me

Never, for anyone, despite my power
This someone can fade away and after change
It won't be me again
And I have to bear with myself for the rest of my life.

Karina Iwaszkiewicz (15)
Danum School Technology College, Doncaster

Dreams

I want to be a doctor
And get A's in my degrees
I want to live a happy life
Grow old with knobbly knees.

We all have our own ambitions
Different or the same
From being rich and famous
To testing video games.

If you're too scared to admit it
Or you don't think you're that clever
Everyone has a special dream
A dream that lasts forever.

Charlotte Utting (13)
Danum School Technology College, Doncaster

Praise Song For My Mother

You are
My eyes for me
You tell me where to go

You are
The stars for me
Bright, shiny, looking down at me.

You are
A lion to me
Big, brave, but graceful.

You are
The pen for me
Can do so much in so little time.

You mean the world to me
So great and powerful, will do anything for me
But you are you as well.

Sophie Croxall (12)
Danum School Technology College, Doncaster

The Punishment

A flick of wind
A flash of light
The blue sky
Went out of sight
The sky turned grey
With a big angry cloud
Everyone silent
The thunder allowed.

The people were punished
For all the bad things
The murders, the stealing
And the greed from the kings
Lightning struck
The world split in two
Craters in the ground
And not just a few

They all crowded round
With a push and a shove
The one who had done this
Was the mighty one above
He pointed His finger
And punished away
The people were praying
On this dreadful day.

The people had been punished
For all things bad
The world was restored
To what it had.

Megan Cooper (13)
Danum School Technology College, Doncaster

The Despair

The despair for those who risked their lives
This is what they say to their mothers
You always somehow make me smile and cheer me up when I'm blue
Life would not be half as nice if I did not have you.

Disappearing towards the battlefield
Memories of home are met with anguish and fear
Fear sinking in that they may not return
Thoughts of loved ones soon have to fade away
As the truck stops!

Here they arrive not knowing the road of death before them
The smiles of their children guiding them
The love of their wives saving them
But sadly not all of them

The soldiers that march on
Bloodstained, limping and vulnerable
Their willpower, hope and determination
Brings them through

In the hours of darkness, waking up to gunshots
The fragrance of bullets hitting the innocent and the smell of rotten flesh
Is unbearable, but the fight must go on
To save us all.

This is war
The surge of rushing blood stops
This is the tragic story of life for the ones who lost theirs
But they did it for the country, not for themselves
And they forced death like predator to prey

So many people lose their lives in war
The one thing that amazes me
Is why did they do it? They did it to save us all
Thank you soldiers for saving the ones that couldn't be
You risked your lives through darkness and death
We won't forget you ever
Leave our hearts never
No matter what happened we'll love you forever.

Emily Johnsen (12)
Danum School Technology College, Doncaster

Cold-Blooded Love!

It's winter
All the snowflakes glitter
Leaves frozen like diamonds
Raindrops frozen like jewels

Chimney smoking
People joking
Sweet lovers' seasons
Calm warming reasons

Cold comfortable love
Flying peaceful dove
Good season for the cold-blooded ones
Vampires increase to tons

The kiss of a vampire
Shall inspire
Lovers' seasons
Filled with desires

My soul within your hands
For all your demands
Love and death
As I felt your breath
Against my cheek
Made me weak.

Tariro Chitiyo (13)
Danum School Technology College, Doncaster

I Am The One

I am the one
Who feels, stiff as a tree
Sometimes because all the glee, just drains out of me
Because I am the one.

I am the one
Who had lots of friends
And my feelings for them just never ends
Because I am the one.

I am the one
Who works really hard
I am the one with my nanna in my heart
Because I am the one.

I am the one
Dark as the deep blue sea
Sometimes I feel open-minded and free
Because I am the one.

I am the one
I am me
I have multicoloured emotions, as you might see
Because, I am me.

Kelsey Douthwaite (12)
Danum School Technology College, Doncaster

Skye!

I don't remember the last time I kissed your forehead
Or the last time I tucked you up in your little, pink, princess bed
All the suffering and pain doesn't come close
It would all be better if time stopped and the world froze
All I need is one precious day to tell you all I need to say
You are the prettiest child, if only the adoption hadn't been filed
All I think of is you, more and more, you're the thing that I adore
I'm not saying your mum failed
I'm just saying every girl deserves a fairy tale.

Tayana Howell (14)
Danum School Technology College, Doncaster

Poem

I thought that you loved me
But I was so wrong
I said that I needed you
And you carried on
I now think you've just given up
Ignored the love
And thrown out the trust.

Then I had this thought inside
It saddened my mind
And ruined my life.

But then I finally realised
Now I see that you're the only one
That's right for me
And now you say you loved
But I have lost
Did you really like me anyway?
And I see you in my dreams at night
And that is where I wish you would be
Because that is where I am and will stay.

Kelsey Courtney (13)
Danum School Technology College, Doncaster

Love

Love is strong, never weak
Helps you out when days are bleak
Love is safe and very warm
Keeps you safe from any storm
Love is like a rainbow
Sometimes stays, sometimes goes
When you're alone no need to hide
Because you have love by your side
I've never felt love before
But when I do, no sadness anymore.

Marie Gibb (12)
Danum School Technology College, Doncaster

Our Dog

Dogs can be cute and fluffy
Dogs can be big and small
But there's only one of our dog
And he's the best of them all.

He's mixed between all sorts of breeds
And runs like the wind
But when it comes to treats
He likes his hot dog sausages tinned.

Our dog's very cute
But not big or small
And there's only one of him
And he's the best of them all.

Rebecca Bosworth (12)
Danum School Technology College, Doncaster

Love

Love is like a flower, always give it the power
To take over your life you may get a wife.

Always stay strong, don't write a love song
Because it's always in your heart, right from the start.

Don't throw it away, cos love is here to stay
Love is very fine and just remember, you will be mine!

Brooke Turner & Emma Hartshorne (13)
Danum School Technology College, Doncaster

War Glory

War is a terrible thing
You can gain glory in war by shooting another man
But you have to carry the guilt that you have killed a human being for all your life
Sometimes with what you've seen
It can make you go mad or insane
Whatever you want to call it
You can get killed in war as well as becoming disabled
Maybe one day you might die by a speeding bullet or a grenade
But one thing is certain
You may get war glory but you might not always like it
War consumes everything like a fire and it will never stop.

Gabriel Carr (11)
Danum School Technology College, Doncaster

The Pork Monster

There was a green dragon from New York
Whose surname was Smarty Chop Port
He worked in a deli
Came home very smelly
Ate dinner, got stabbed with a fork!

Kyle Kirkland (14)
Ellesmere College (Secondary Special School), Leicester

The Silly Poem

There was a bad monster from Birmingham
That killed a short knight with a yam
Pushed the yam in his mouth
The yam travelled south
The monster made yam into jam!

Uzair Suleman (13)
Ellesmere College (Secondary Special School), Leicester

The Monster

I heard a noise at the dusty door
It sounded like a lion's roar
I went upstairs and there appeared
A scary shadow I had feared!

Then a voice lit up all the lights
Leaving me with a fearsome fright
So I made my way up the stiff stairs
Where there I saw a trail of hairs!

I went forward a bit more
And there I saw a ferocious claw
Before I could move it pinched my toes
I made my way to the rusty roof
Where there I lost a precious tooth.

I turned around and saw a monster
It was a . . . huge, orange, hairy lobster!

Adeela Ahmed (11)
Fir Vale Secondary School, Sheffield

Red Rose

Red rose, red rose
Roses are red like strawberries
Its smell like autumn leaves
It is beautiful as a puppy
Red rose, red rose
Where are you?
Where can you be?
I want to see you
They grow in dirty
Soil and turn into summer flowers
Red rose, red rose
They only blossom in spring and summer
Leaving the autumn and winter behind
Red rose, red rose.

Htet Htet Khaing Win (13)
Fir Vale Secondary School, Sheffield

Friendship

Friendship always matters, even if it shatters
It always starts off with a smile,
Doesn't matter about looks or style
It may begin with a rickety start
But later on it'll sound all smart
You always expect them to care for you
And always be there to help you through
Friendship always depends on honesty and trust
Without these two your friendship will go bust
Betraying, lying to your friends may sound OK
But it's got to end
Keep your friendship as strong as steel
And maybe one day you can use it as a shield.

Nagina Shahzadi (11)
Fir Vale Secondary School, Sheffield

I Am A Refugee!

The shooting has started, we are on our way
From leaving this country we might come back one day
Leaving our family and friends to suffer, I don't want to leave
I want to stay, want to help my family
Through this hard time of day
I feel we cannot survive
But if we stick together we will never die
This is a poem on me, a refugee
It's like being nothing, no one can see you in night or day
I am a piece of wood, waiting to rot away.

Farrah Din (12)
Fir Vale Secondary School, Sheffield

Flames, Smoke, Ash

The stadium was alive with high spirits
As people watched for the winning team
As people prayed as they were awfully keen.

But among the cheers a scream broke out
Followed on by a bellowing shout.

The stand was engulfed by flames and smoke
As people started to flee as they choked.

Now the flames and smoke were just a blur
As people's minds started to whirr.

Even though people's bodies are gone
Their souls still remain
As you cannot rub out this treacherous stain.

As the press finish their piece
A horde of ambulances come,
Piling in bodies, two in every one.

And now the flames, smoke, ash and bodies are gone
The stadium rebuilt, people's loved ones return
As they feel like a scared child hiding under his quilt.

Ashly Millward (13)
Humphrey Perkins High School, Barrow Upon Soar

A Loving Husband

A loving husband
A darling wife
They wanted to live together
They wanted to share their life.

But he was a cheater
And she was in danger
He had a secret lover
It couldn't get any stranger.

When she found out
They started a row
She threatened to leave him
He hit her hard, but he's sorry now.

He hit her with a griddle pan
The blow struck to her head
He put her in the freezer
That way no one would know she was dead.

A man killed his wife
The Old Bailey heard
No one would have wanted this
A divorce would've been preferred.

They heard he put her in the freezer
She was in there for three years
He just slobbed around the house
Drinking without fears.

On a fateful Wednesday
Not too long ago
The binman could not move one bin
He found her dead body, he paced to and fro.

So now he has been put in jail
He got a life sentence
He is locked in prison
Shut behind a fence.

Jake Gant (13)
Humphrey Perkins High School, Barrow Upon Soar

Raspadskaya Mine Explosion

Mine president

I was sitting in my office
When I heard a monstrous bang
I turned towards the window
As the alarm began to clang.

Miner

The people near the surface
Were scrambling straight out
Survival of the fittest
Would we ever get out?

Mine president

We watched them clamber down
With faces full of fear
Whose stupid idea was this?
We had to get everyone clear.

Miner

The rescuers were coming
They slid down lifeline ropes
The rocks began to tumble
Just like our brave hopes.

Mine president

What's happened to the miners
The ones we sent below?
Or the rescuers that followed
Will we ever know?

Miner

They sucked away our lifeblood
As the shaft, it had collapsed
We died from lack of oxygen
That, we never grasped.

Mine president

When you ask me if I feel guilty
The answer's surely yes
For I murdered all those people
And sent them to their deaths.

Emma Haynes (13)
Humphrey Perkins High School, Barrow Upon Soar

Election 2010

Thursday 6th of May
The day of the futile Election
Time for the party leaders
To face hope and rejection.

The queues at the polling stations
Were like a meandering river
And not everybody got to vote
For who they though would deliver.

The polling stations swallowed the public up
Just like food and digested our opinions
And said it tasted good.

Disgust and anguish in Brown's lack of leadership
And his power, like water, is not a river
But a tap that drips.

Victim to this endless combat
David Cameron thought No 10 was his
That he could repair a broken economy
And so did the Conservatives.

The Liberal Democrats did as we expected
And formed a coalition with the Conservatives
So as not to be rejected
But maybe in six months
There'll be another Election
And maybe in six months
They'll face hope and rejection.

Josiah Williamson (13)
Humphrey Perkins High School, Barrow Upon Soar

Ballad Of The SAS

As I arrive I start to train
I start to sweat and bleed with pain
I'm here to train to go to Iraq
In my camouflage of green and black.

My second step of training is to climb the hill
Doing this takes stamina and will
Finally I'm flown off to Iraq
In my camouflage of green and black.

The officer says, 'Hit the deck.'
Otherwise a bullet goes through your neck
I think I'm going to die in Iraq
In my camouflage of green and black.

I have to shut off my emotions, I have to do it now
Now I'm really worried because I really don't know how
I will die for my country in Iraq
In my camouflage of green and black.

Now the adrenaline's pumping, going through my veins
If I get shot I doubt I will feel pain
I'm getting angry in Iraq
In my camouflage of green and black.

I think of my family back at home
I don't want to die and leave them all alone
I'm thinking of my family in Iraq
In my camouflage of green and black.

I feel really guilty, my squadron has blown up
Now off their dead bodies I clean off all the muck
I sit next to the coffins coming home from Iraq
In my camouflage of green and black.

I say don't send the troops in
To a war we cannot win.

Daniel Hart (13)
Humphrey Perkins High School, Barrow Upon Soar

The Election

When Tony Blair could do no more
He felt it was time to step down
The Chancellor of the Exchequer took on the role
Of Prime Minister, Gordon Brown.

The sixth of May just an ordinary day
But this year an election loomed
Lots of campaigning went on through the weeks
But which parties were set to be doomed?

Registration cards were sent
To people of the nation
From 7am till 10pm
You could vote at the polling station.

No one got the majority votes
For Conservatives it was disaster
So talks were held in Number 10
To decide the government faster.

Finally a decision was made
For two parties to unite
The Lib Dems and Conservatives
Would together fight for their rights.

So now Gordon Brown could no longer win
He felt it was time to go
His time in charge had come to an end
He'd put on a pretty good show.

So automatically Cameron had won
The Queen confirmed his stand
With a chat and a joke, the deal was done
Sealed with a 'kissing of hands'.

David Cameron took on the role of sorting the new Cabinet
Clegg was declared the deputy, now can Britain get out of debt?

Megan Barston (13)
Humphrey Perkins High School, Barrow Upon Soar

The Heroes Of The White House

The attack on the 9th of September
It was an organised disaster
But not many people remember
The heroes of the White House.

For there were two other attacks
On that grave and sad day
As the people in New York heard a mighty crash!
But not the White House, for that flight had heroes.

The Towers, Pentagon and White House
Were targeted like cat and mouse
But not a plane came near the White House
Because the White House had heroes.

The call was recorded
As a hero phoned his wife
His love was given
Before the heroes of the White House went to stop the flight.

They charged across the plane
As Arthur charged his knights
But as soon as the terrorists heard bustling, they stopped the flight
For the heroes of the White House were charging towards them.

They aimed the plane towards the ground
The jets on full
The farmers heard a mighty pound
But it never reached the White House, thanks to the heroes.

The White House still stands from day to night
But not a hero lived to see their loved ones or wives
The heroes of the White House on that dark and disastrous flight
I will always remember and I will never forget.

The heroes of the White House
And how their deaths were met.

George Mitchell (13)
Humphrey Perkins High School, Barrow Upon Soar

Drizzle The One And Only

In the south of Gloucestershire
Drizzle was born into the life of royalty
Trotting on his own four legs
He treated his owner with love and loyalty.

Growing up in the royal gardens
Drizzle had found his true home
His heart belonged to Harry
And he never felt alone.

The very special day had come
He felt extremely proud
Drizzle was ready for polo
He looked out to the massive crowd.

People were cheering like animals in a zoo
Shouting loudly with joy
Big, cheesy, smiling faces
On every girl and boy.

The horses got ready
Lined up in their numbered box
As quick as a bullet shot
Bang, they were running as fast as a fox.

Drizzle was a sprinting machine
As he was running rapidly round
But something went terribly wrong
As his legs plummeted to the ground.

Drizzle suffered a fatal heart attack
As he was rushed away from the game
The stadium's heart was broken
And Harry's life will never be the same

Rest in peace Drizzle
You will never be forgotten.

Emily Fox (13)
Humphrey Perkins High School, Barrow Upon Soar

Brits Trapped In Bangkok

The sound of bullets and bombs everywhere
It was a live fire zone
Once were a happy couple
Now the holiday was blown
Brits trapped in Bangkok.

Capital crashes to the ground
People are dropping like flies
The once calm city turns to horror
As people say their last goodbyes.

Death toll rises to 31
The British think they are next
As the guns go bang!
They send their last text.

A protester cries out to them
Tells them to get away
He falls to the ground with a smash
Seeing the last of today.

The seriousness of it hits them
The Brits are in harm's way
There's crashing all around them
With nowhere to get away.

As the last of the protesters are gunned down
Screaming as they go
The British know they will not escape
As they have no friend, only foe.

Blown bodies cover Bangkok
The British are long gone
Bodies scatter streets like snow
They died singing the song
'Brits trapped in Bangkok'.

Renaise Carter (13)
Humphrey Perkins High School, Barrow Upon Soar

No To Cuts! No To Closures!

Bang! The door is shut
For teenagers trying for uni
Like adults pushing through the line
Taking the opportunity
No to cuts! No to closures!

Angry adults losing their jobs
Due to the recession
But they have enough money
To get a better education
No to cuts! No to closures!

To definitely go to uni
Teenagers pay seven grand a year
This is why they protest
'It's miles too dear!'
No to cuts! No to closures!

'Why does it have to happen?'
'Why does it happen here?'
For the unlucky teenagers
Trying for uni, in Leicestershire
No to cuts! No to closures!'

They can do it, Clegg and Cameron
To get the problem solved
They can do it, Clegg and Cameron
To get more involved
No to cuts! No to closures!

There is a moral
In the ballad today
That the young, smart teenagers
Just have to pay
No to cuts! No to closures!

Connor Higgins (13)
Humphrey Perkins High School, Barrow Upon Soar

Bring Back Millie

Liam was in a world of his own
He never spoke a word
No sentence, no syllable
What these thieves have done is unfair and absurd
And now she's gone.

She made him happy
His 'dog' and his 'mummy'
Were his first and only words
But now his life doesn't seem so sunny
And now she's gone.

His grandad saved up his pension
900 pounds to be exact
Nothing could replace her
No horse, no rat, no cat
And now she's gone.

He'd bang on her cage
Screaming inside
Tears roll down his face like drops of pain
The ones he could no longer hide
And how she's gone.

It was from the garden they took her
The little petite pup
Now they have wasted
All that saving up
And now she's gone.

Hopefully she will turn up
That sweet playful pup
So lonely little Liam
Can finally hold his chin up
But for now she's gone.

Katie Marie Westmacott (13)
Humphrey Perkins High School, Barrow Upon Soar

Corner Shop Robbery

Six weeks ago
A robbery was made
They stole two crates of beer
Niraj Samani was afraid.

A robbery was made six weeks ago
The police have reacted very slow.

Two men came in
That people don't know
They put down the security shutters
But the police have failed to catch the duo.

A robbery was made six weeks ago
The police have reacted very slow.

Niraj's shop has been burgled three times
Within the last ten years
So now the owner works in fear
Even though he sells cheap beers.

A robbery was made six weeks ago
The police have reacted very slow.

Niraj is very upset, he thinks he should go
Six weeks on, the police still don't know.

A robbery was made six weeks ago
The police have reacted very slow.

He called the police, said
He'd been robbed
Also threatened with a pair of scissors
Niraj's family was scared and sobbed.

A robbery was made six weeks ago
The police still don't know.

Kyle Archer (13)
Humphrey Perkins High School, Barrow Upon Soar

The Cold-Hearted Thugs

The innocent man
Was left lying on the ground
They left in a hurry
Leaving no one around.

After being pounded many times
They drove away not caring at all
They left him lying on the double yellow lines
From the first strike of the bat they watched him fall.

The ambulance was called
The details were took
And shortly after that
It was written in the big black book.

The ambulance arrived
He was swiftly picked up
And in a hurry
To the hospital he was took.

A few stitches here
And a few stitches there
His face was messed up
Like a complete nightmare.

The investigation began
The evidence was found
The cold-hearted thugs
Were sent to the ground.

They were found guilty
The man survived
They got what was coming
The man was revived
And of their freedom the thugs were deprived.

Siân Lloyd-McLear (13)
Humphrey Perkins High School, Barrow Upon Soar

Sheep Attack

Sitting on the shores of magnificent Rutland
Lay many dozens of sheep
Helplessly they stay
Stuck inside the wooden keep.

No matter how much money
The owners have to pay
Even the nice dogs
Attack their calm, worthless prey.

Owners think their dogs are just playing
Forcing the sheep to flee into the water
Her fluffy coat got waterlogged
But no one could have caught her.

Bang! goes the shot
Put the sheep out of its misery
The evil dogs invaded
Why should sheep be hurt and left dizzy?

1,000 ewes and 2,000 lambs
Half were left for dead
When the sun comes out so do the dogs
The farmers full of dread.

It's not hard to go somewhere else
Just leave the sheep in peace
One animal can cause so much mayhem
When they should be on a leash.

Unusually quiet
Sheep lay frozen on the ground
Once the farmer had realised
He was left distraught by what he had found.

Heidi Mumford (13)
Humphrey Perkins High School, Barrow Upon Soar

The Haiti Disaster

It was a lovely day
The sun it was so bright
Haiti was not ready
For something unknown to their sight.

Suddenly an earthquake began
Panicking people everybody screaming
This awful quake was getting worse
It was so scary, what was its meaning?

Haiti was in ruins
Buildings falling down
Sandcastles in the sea
Destroying this lovely town.

People were dying out
As if they were in a plague
Two hundred and thirty thousand dead
The help was so vague.

So many people were trapped
Crash from underground
For them it was so scary
Like dogs in a pound.

Lots of rescuers came
Many medical teams
Engineers and communicators
Bringing funds and scaffolding beams.

Our thoughts are with the families
The ones of the dead
The three million that were affected
The ones without a bed.

Amy Walker (12)
Humphrey Perkins High School, Barrow Upon Soar

The Haiti Disaster

The sun was shining high in the sky
Attracting tourists like food to a fly
The waves roll onto the beach
With the sunset becoming out of reach.

The next day the sun didn't rise
As dark clouds and lightning filled the skies
The people of Haiti were in for a shock
As their clock would tick but never again tock.

Street lamps flickered and pylons started to shake
This was the beginning of the unforgiving quake
People flooded onto the streets
Trampling on the road with their bare feet.

The buildings collapsed all around
As every structure fell to the ground
The news reporters pounced on their culture
Like an unfed vulture.

Rescue workers from all around
Fled to the disaster ground
Panic and worry filled the air
And a woman screams in despair.

Trapped in rubble, struggling for life
An old crippled man searching for his wife
The earthquake has caused a lot of damage
Who knows if they'll ever manage.

The people here have had it rough
And the rescuers have done enough
The people of Haiti will never be the same
And Mother Nature is to blame.

Harry Smith (13)
Humphrey Perkins High School, Barrow Upon Soar

Britain's Scorcher

Spring is here
Nearly summer
Hot enough for all
Definitely no bummer.

Unlike last year
This was warm
People fled to the sea
Like a human storm.

People were boiling
Burning throughout
But in the sea
Children would shout.

For their mothers
They were red
Burning hot
To shade they fled.

It wasn't all bad
Some used cream
Everyone loved the weather
A British dream.

The sun was blazing
High above in the sky
Midday struck
Some would fly

Faraway
To a foreign place
Warmer they are
What a disgrace.

Joshua Gregory (13)
Humphrey Perkins High School, Barrow Upon Soar

Magic Mermaid Girl

She was born as strong as a pearl
Even though she was
Quite different to a usual girl
She stayed confident with a zest for life.

Friends say 'she had a great 10 years'
People stood by her
To take away the dreaded tears
She stayed confident with a zest for life.

Even though she had this condition
She enjoyed her life
Like she was on a fierce mission
She stayed confident with a zest for life.

She was like a tiger fighting
The way she kept strong
Shiloh was bright like lightning
She stayed confident with a zest for life.

For a week she went to a camp
She was excited
But she never forgot her night camp
She stayed confident with a zest for life.

Unfortunately Shiloh died
At the age of ten
As her poor family cried
She stayed confident with a zest for life.

Though she was so different to us
Her heart was as warm
She was strong, never made a fuss
She stayed confident with a zest for life.

Hannah Brooks (13)
Humphrey Perkins High School, Barrow Upon Soar

Making Music

Sitting in a dressing room
Excitement in the air
We're all waiting for the call
Instruments everywhere.

In groups of friends we sit and chat
Laughing and joking together
Minstrels, sandwiches and sweets
We'll remember this night forever.

We queue silently backstage
Then smile as we walk on
My heart's pounding, the lights are blinding
Worried it will all go wrong.

The floor seems so far away
As I walk down the formidable space
The anonymous audience stare back at me
And our fingers begin to race.

Lost in music, it's what we love
Performing to the public like this
Months of Saturday morning rehearsals
All for this moment of bliss.

Exhilaration when it's over
I can't believe what I've done
I've just performed at De Montford Hall
And there's more concerts like that to come.

Sixty-two years of Leicestershire Arts
An outstanding creative service
But the council funding is being cut
Will we be able to carry on learning?

Elizabeth Wells (13)
Humphrey Perkins High School, Barrow Upon Soar

The Guitar God

1963, music was tedious
And inspiration was rare
Nobody dared to stand out
There was no flair.

Until all of a sudden
From out of the blue
God came down from Heaven
And stepped forth as Jimi, overdue.

So Hendrix humbly shuffled
Out onto the imposing stage
When he started to play his guitar
The crowd was truly amazed.

And now came his solo
Oh such a beautiful melody
The birds stopped singing to listen
And the crowd went silent expectantly.

Jimi took off his Stratocaster
Then he set it alight
His fingers of fire burned the neck
The crowd roared in delight.

Jimi, the greatest guitarist
Of all the universe and time
Yet he took the dangerous drugs
And paid for committing his crimes.

Because on September 18th 1970
The tragic news slowly unfurled
Jimi Hendrix was dead
And so was the poor world.

Katie Macdonald (13)
Humphrey Perkins High School, Barrow Upon Soar

Icelandic Volcano

On the 20th of March
Two thousand and ten
An Icelandic volcano
Started to erupt again.

It previously happened
In eighteen twenty-one
When the very same volcano
Drew a circle around the sun.

A giant swarm of ash
Flew across the sky
All the British airlines
Were unable to fly.

The disaster left many stranded
In a place they did not know well
Without accommodation or money
Their Heaven turned into Hell.

As no planes were flying
For some the sky was clear
We couldn't see the ash
Up with the atmosphere.

The volcano continued to smoke
For a week and then
When everyone thought it was over
The ash covered Britain again.

We should never underestimate
Mother Nature's awesome powers
She can coat the world with ash
Then cover it with flowers.

Richard Palmer (13)
Humphrey Perkins High School, Barrow Upon Soar

League One Play-Off Semi-Final

Charlton vs Swindon
20,000 fans await
The play-off semi-final
17th May is the date.

Who will be legends?
Wembley is the prize
But who will be losers
With tears in their eyes?

An own goal is the opener
Twenty-eight minutes gone
The crowd as wild as animals
It is now game on.

Half-time approaches
And Charlton makes it two
David Mooney with the glorious goal
The manager says phew.

Danny Ward scores
Swindon are back from the dead
The score's now level
Penalties is where we head.

The penalty shoot-out starts
Swindon score all five
Charlton miss their second
Their dreams are no longer alive.

Swindon are the legends
Wembley is their prize
Charlton are the losers
With tears in their eyes.

Nathan Munden (13)
Humphrey Perkins High School, Barrow Upon Soar

Election, Election

The election was about to start
Among the people there was some talk
About who would win
And who would walk.

Would Labour win again
Like the last 13 years
Or would David Cameron win
With his fellow Conservative peers?

Everyone looked nervous
Conservatives were in the lead
Watching Nicky Morgan
Just beating Andy Reed.

The people of Britain voted
Conservatives had most seats
Lib Dems joined the Tories
And Labour accepted defeat.

There was a change in the country
On 10 Downing Street
In the Prime Minister's office
Would walk someone else's feet.

Brown quit as Prime Minister
Resignation accepted by the Queen
What will happen now?
Would Cameron get his dream?

In walked David Cameron
Willing and so keen
Ready to fight for his country
And serve his royal Queen.

Jake Samardzija (13)
Humphrey Perkins High School, Barrow Upon Soar

Election Ballad

The clock struck seven
The race began
They tripped and stumbled
As they ran and ran.

The doors were like a monster
Hungry for its food
People were still flooding in
In a highly confused mood.

The box was crossed
I could do no more
All I could do was wait
Oh, it would be such a bore.

A Hung Parliament was announced
The dreaded final count
They wondered and wondered about
Who was in and who was out.

Minds racing, finding a way
To make all this voting work
Number 10 became very busy
As camera men began to lurk.

'EastEnders' was cancelled
The long awaited news instead
The joining of two parties
Meant that the country had a head.

The job was now taken
We knew who had won
The shaking of hands
Revealed it was David Cameron.

Beth Rennocks (13)
Humphrey Perkins High School, Barrow Upon Soar

The Bradford Fire

A Saturday afternoon
On the 11th of May
Many people lost their lives
It was a horrific day.

The sun was beaming over the stands
And everyone was cheering
They didn't want their team to lose
But that's all they were fearing.

Suddenly there was a scream
And no one even breathed
Even the football players stopped
Losing goals they could have achieved.

And then the whole pitch was screaming
Fearing for their lives
Running about like angry bees
When someone shakes their hive.

Children lost their beloved parents
Scared and all alone
They didn't know who'd be there
If they finally got back home.

Suddenly a gap appeared in the fence
And everyone was filled with hope
People scrambled and pushed to get out
But the weaker could not cope.

That one cigarette was a murderer
it killed fifty-six people
But now the family of the dead
Walk under the church steeple.

Hannah Greatrex (13)
Humphrey Perkins High School, Barrow Upon Soar

Bradford Blazing Ballad

Mexican waves rolled around
Just like the rapid moving sea
Celebrations for the Cup filled the air
But it was a terrible place to be.

People started smelling scary smoke
As it rose from the stands round the game
This match would go down in history
This match would become fame.

Screams and panic filled the air
As the fire spread further and further
People getting burnt and battered
This fire was a murderer.

The wooden stands started to collapse
Onto the pitch which then caught fire
The heart of the stadium was ablaze
It was time for the place to retire.

People searched for their family
Found some dead, some alive
The deceased are loved, but lonely
Would anybody survive?

The newsflash hit the TV
Families watched in fear
Flickering flames, searing heat
Seeing children filled with tears.

Overall this match was a disaster
The game was never won
Families are ruined and lonely
Lives are dead and gone.

Sam Johnson (13)
Humphrey Perkins High School, Barrow Upon Soar

The Bus Ride Disaster

The summer exams are finally over
We jumped into the air and let out a scream
Now we're going to have so much fun
Like a crazy, crazy dream.

'Is this the way to Alton Towers?
All the rides are scaring me silly
Dreaming dreams of Alton Towers
And our guide called Milly.'

Slipping on the icy road as the bus driver loses control
The bus begins to slither around, drunk of fuel
With a crash and a boom they fell into the lake
Bringing them out on this cold day, who would be such a fool?

Deep down ten feet underwater
Unexpectedly now nobody was safe
Shouting, screeching, shouting, screaming
People underneath the bus began to chafe.

Like a mass murderer on the hunt
Hunting down, then. Finding a jackpot
Bodies and hearts forever broken
Now what has everyone got?

Dragging people out from under the bus
One girl dead and all with serious injuries
Two air-lifted to the hospital
Others sent to different houses like evacuees.

Nothing has yet been decided
But could that snowy blanket that lay
Have been that humble destroyer
That ruined everyone's perfect day.

Hannah Hickinbotham (13)
Humphrey Perkins High School, Barrow Upon Soar

Craig Kieswetter Vs South Africa

Craig Kieswetter wasn't able to play for his country
Not even one match
They went for somebody else
But he's England's best catch.

In the last match
The ball was as battered as a fish
Crash, bang, wallop!
He served up a delightful dish.

He's playing them tomorrow
For the lion's mane
The country South Africa
They can't win the game.

The Kensington Oval
A lovely ground
England made it to this stage
In one great bound.

During last December
'Yes, I want him back,'
Said the South African skipper
To Kieswetter that's cack.

He'll carry on playing for England
Making the crowd go wild
Hitting huge sixes
In his own style.

He is a brilliant batsman
Like all the greats
The opener and keeper
He's opened England's gates.

Nathan Preston (13)
Humphrey Perkins High School, Barrow Upon Soar

The Ballad Of Haiti's Hurt

The city lay still and sleeping
But alert was in the air
Glistening waves rippled lightly
There was no sound, not a care.

Suddenly people felt uneasy
They knew something was wrong
As the ground started to shake
They realised they didn't have long.

Frantic shouts were everywhere
The chaos was immense
Buildings, hospitals and schools
Collapsed like a crooked fence.

Haiti was in destruction
Dead bodies lying like rotten apples
Everyone was crying
It looked like a lost battle.

The stench of death hung in the air
No one was free from pain
Pain from losing a loved one
Hope would never be the same.

Single salty teardrops
Fell down one child's face
It was like a huge jigsaw
Putting back the pieces, trying to win the race.

The awful worldwide disaster
That made Haiti go boom
Rebuilding the city again
Unravelling new life like a revived cocoon.

Megan Hunter (12)
Humphrey Perkins High School, Barrow Upon Soar

The Ballad Of Eyjafjallajokul

In the land of waterfalls
Where geysers reach the sky
Above the jagged rock formations
Crowds of seabirds fly.

Around the base of the volcano
Where the fishing village stood
There now is nothing but some ash
And blackened, burning wood.

A stream of lava slowly oozed
Out of the smoking crater
But Icelandic people didn't know
It would erupt again soon later.

The cloud of ash it spread about
Above the ocean blue
And high above the Atlantic
The ash cloud swelled and grew.

As planes flew past the growing cloud
The ash blocked up the jet
And while the pilots panicked quietly
A new order was set.

The planes should touch down on the airstrip
And none should leave the ground
All transatlantic flights were cancelled
As the tourists soon found.

A week later in all the airports
The ban was dropped in vain
For as the angry mountain booms
The story starts again.

Sam Mottram (13)
Humphrey Perkins High School, Barrow Upon Soar

A Race For Power

It is the 6th of May again
And parliament has to change
Gordon Brown has to step aside
It has to be rearranged.

Voters charged like raging bulls
To the polling stations
As if they were bright red rags
They lived up to their expectations.

Voting cards stared at voters
With growing eager excitement
The fact that parliament might change
Gave them great enjoyment.

Everyone has voted
And yet parliament is hung
Determination is spreading
The tedious war has just begun.

With the winning Conservatives
Stands faithful David Cameron
Who to make sure he is the one they agree with
Will run any marathon.

Gordon Brown's petrol tank
Slowly ran out of fuel
He retired just before the end
And ended his long-lasting rule.

After parliament came to its decision
The Queen was alerted once more
She and David sealed the deal
Ending the political war.

Emily Bacon (12)
Humphrey Perkins High School, Barrow Upon Soar

The Police Strike

A strike, a strike!
The police are on strike
Something the public
Do not like.

Once we went into debt
All the forces dropped back
Now we're looking for who's to blame
And who's to get the sack.

But now news has spread
All across the nation
That the one to blame
Is the police federation.

But in my opinion
It's not you see
The police did nothing
The government sent money overseas.

To feed wars and get more power
Whilst the police get cut
It seems that Britain's police force
Is stuck in a rut.

Crime is on the rise
And police are on the fall
Britain needs to act
Before we lose it all.

Peace is what we want
And peace is what we need
The police are as restrained
As a dog on a lead.

Aiden McWeeney (13)
Humphrey Perkins High School, Barrow Upon Soar

Icelandic Volcano Eruption

An Icelandic volcano erupted
On the 20th March 2010
Thousands of flights were cancelled
The ash caused tragic mayhem.

Many people were trapped abroad
Unable to come back
Assorted airlines were in trouble
Many staff were sacked.

A gigantic black shadow
Invaded the vast sky
Causing everything to halt
That was occurring up high.

Ferries and taxis were the only options
For people trying to get home
This wouldn't be necessary
If the flights hadn't been postponed.

The ash has been like a black sheet
Rising over the continent
It's as if there was an evil God
That had made sure it was sent.

Eventually the ash began to clear away
So it wasn't a total disaster
The evenings revealed spectacular sunsets
And transportation finally moved faster.

For now the trauma is over
The ash has gone away
But there is a chance it could erupt again
Causing this catastrophe to return, one day.

Joe Darling (13)
Humphrey Perkins High School, Barrow Upon Soar

The Oil Rig Disaster

Not every story told
Always finishes the same
Some endings are unhappy
And that is a terrible shame.

And the story I shall tell
Will not differ from this code
The first to see was a fisherman
As across the sea he rowed.

At first there was a screeching noise
Like a whistling in a room
Just like a rusty old steam train
And then a loud *boom, boom, boom!*

Eleven people sadly died
As lifeless as a granite stone
As they're left to roam the Underworld
But will be doing so alone.

The sealife was still suffering
Then experts said they knew what to do
They made this metal monster
But would it ultimately fail too?

The families of the dead
Were still grieving as you would
They asked questions, 'Why were our friends killed?'
And why the shores were stained with blood

The problem will be sorted
But most likely not today
The question is will it be too late
Before the sealife dies away?

Owen Chamberlain (12)
Humphrey Perkins High School, Barrow Upon Soar

Bradford Ballad

The fans arrived at Bradford
For some it would be their last game
Not knowing the Division 3 title
Wouldn't be the centre of fame.

The fire started at the main stand
The fans were struggling and trying
To escape the terrible blaze
Which was becoming more petrifying.

Within four minutes it was gone
And so were the people inside
This was terrifyingly bad
They knew there was nowhere to hide.

Loved ones were on their mind
People searching and crying
Pushing through the crowds
Who were watching the stadium frying.

Witnesses trembled with fear
Police and ambulance aid
The injured and the disturbed
The pain and misery it's made.

The fires are now controlled
The dead are now counted
The lonely crying like waterfalls
The press are getting excited.

The fans begin to gather
Reluctant to be there
Reluctant to remember
But they know they have to be fair.

James Harman-Thomas (13)
Humphrey Perkins High School, Barrow Upon Soar

The Miracle

Yesterday at 2.25
A little boy escaped with his life
When the A330 did a dive
Straight towards its doom.

Many people died that day
Many people were upset that day
All the bodies just lay
Silent and dead.

The people weren't ready to die
But one boy escaped with his life
When the police heard a cry
From within the rubble.

His only injury was a broken leg
But he was in a lot of shock
As he just lost his lovely dad Greg
Who was his only parent.

The plane went crash
When it heavily hit the ground
The police came in a dash
But only one survived.

Debris covered the runway like snow
Dead people lay there burning away
They piled the bodies in a row
While the smoke filled the sky.

No one knows what happened that day
But the police know they won't forget
When they saw all the bodies lay
Dead and silent.

Robert Shuttlewood (13)
Humphrey Perkins High School, Barrow Upon Soar

The 30 Man England World Cup

It's time for the stars to take to the stage
As we have heard cool Capello's voice
Will they be known as legends?
This is these fantastic footballer's choice.

By June there will be cheers and joy
Who will have jubilance in their eyes?
As from now their dazzling dreams will be nothing but
Thoughts of the glistening prize.

But for many there is catastrophe
What about those left behind?
Like the wing wizard Young
Capello must have lost his marvellous mind.

Wayne Rooney, the king is the hope
Will he show his might?
Let the crazy crowd go wild
England's eyes shine big at the sight.

So many have given it all
Zeus-like for the Prem
At times elegant like an eagle
Now can these god-gifted show their men?

But quality comes in more than 30
Exiled from the squad was Carlton Cole
Ecstatic like they've won it already are so many
Although it's so tragic some have lost their soul.

The nation's passion is thunderous
Like they're fighting for their life every nation tries
But only 11 can live the dream
23 days until we hear many cries.

Joseph Myko (12)
Humphrey Perkins High School, Barrow Upon Soar

The Election

The election was all over
And the people had chose
Who would rule their country
The Conservative party rose.

Conservative and Labour were neck and neck
But Cameron won by a majority
The people of Britain voted
And those who won have the country's authority.

Labour ruled for 13 years
And Gordon lasted for three
Labour had won a few less votes
And in went the Tory party.

Lib Dems had negotiated
They had chosen their side
They teamed up with Conservative
And Labour's chance passed by.

The LD and Clegg decided
David Cameron shook the Queen's hand
But when he left the palace

Cameron was at Downing Street
Standing at Number 10's door
He gave his first proper speech
With cameras wanting more.

The Election was close
But Labour's votes were thinner
After his first speech
David Cameron was a winner.

Harvey Gaunt (13)
Humphrey Perkins High School, Barrow Upon Soar

The Ballad Of Drizzle's Disaster

A lovely sunny and warm day
Perfect for a polo match
Their minds are blank, their hearts are set
Soon to come is a deathly catch.

Here is Harry on his horse
The crowds stand up and cheer
They sit back down on their chairs
And in two minutes they fill with fear.

Drizzle, as proud as ever
Carried out Harry with pride
But unfortunately soon to come
His precious life was subtly starting to hide.

The horses lined up nervous as mice
Shuffling their feet, ready for the game
Harry, William and Prince Charles' lives
Will never be the same.

Harry and Drizzle run like the wind
Hitting the ball they ran, they ran
Poor old Drizzle is struggling
They take him away as fast as they can.

Drizzle withers like a flower
Stone-cold dead on the floor
A heart attack. Drizzle dying, dead
We won't see him anymore.

Poor old Harry, his heart ripped and torn
The love of his life, smashed like a pot
All will be OK, but we will miss him a lot.

Alice Lees (13)
Humphrey Perkins High School, Barrow Upon Soar

Explosion Destroys The Deep Water Horizon Rig!

Crackles of thunder and lightning; lurking
Raindrops fall to the ground as if they are tears of pain and sorrow
The almost silent, cool breeze blows against my face
The sea throws waves of fury, which will die tomorrow.

I feel all alone and deserted, in this vast and secluded area of the Atlantic Ocean
The starlight is not reflecting in the above night sky
The ground beneath my feet, begins to slightly shake and tremble with fear
I prepare to say my final goodbye.

Silence echoes throughout the Deep Water Horizon rig
Shivers are being sent along the back of my spine, I come to a halt
My hairs are standing upright upon my neck
My heart begins to rapidly pound, I know it is my fault …

The situation begins to dawn upon me
I know deep within my heart that I should not be out here,
that this is just a mistake
Not so late at night
This is no joke, it was no fake.

Boom! An explosion rises, with ferocity and vengeance
Right before my very eyes
Autumn-coloured flames and puffs of clouds of smoke
This was unexpected and no lie.

I mean, it must have been an accident, what else could it be?
Eleven workers have lost their lives
It should never have happened
Only a mere few have survived.

Paige Hewes (13)
Humphrey Perkins High School, Barrow Upon Soar

England Win ICC World Twenty20 Cup

England and Australia
Go out to play
While the batsmen are here to stay
For the remainder of the day.

People buy tickets
To watch England take wickets
While the batsmen are here to stay
For the remainder of the day.

Like a bolt of lightning
The ball thundered through the air
While they clock up runs at a pace quite frightening
The batsmen are here to stay
For the remainder of the day.

Kevin Pietersen smashed it out the ground
While he ran down the wicket in several great bounds
The batsmen are here to stay
For the remainder of the day.

The ball was as battered as a fish
While the England boys wish
The batsmen are here to stay
For the remainder of the day.

The England boys had won
Tonight they will have fun
While the batsmen are here to stay
For the remainder of the day.

Max Ratcliffe (13)
Humphrey Perkins High School, Barrow Upon Soar

The Libya Jet Crash

People board the Afriqiyah flight
The people sit and rest their head
Plane began to take off
One alive, one hundred and three dead.

The plane is soaring in the air
'What a wonderful flight to Tripoli,' someone on the plane said.
Flying over many seas
One alive, one hundred and three dead.

The plane approached the Tripoli runway
People using the chairs as their bed
But the plane crashed just short of the runway
One alive, one hundred and three dead.

As the plane started to tip
Nearer to the ground the plane sped
The plane banged to the solid floor
One alive, one hundred and three dead.

The boy was ejected into the air
Pain rapidly rushing through his head
Bits off the plane floated down like confetti
One alive, one hundred and three dead.

The families who lost their beloved ones
All happened to have said
It was a tragic day
With one alive, one hundred and three dead.

Christian Warren (13)
Humphrey Perkins High School, Barrow Upon Soar

The Ballad Of Haiti

The winding wind twisting round and round
As the thunder clouds barked
Lightning bolts ripped off the ground
While the sky above them sparked.

The quivering quake began to shake
In wobbling houses open cracks split
Stone-built buildings began to crumble
Haiti reduced to an empty pit.

Shouts of fright and fear
Baby children trapped under the rubble
Everybody there shared the same thought
The overall deaths began to double.

The bleeding heart of the mangled mess
Haiti filled with shame
Population considerably less
That day the earthquake came.

Terrified parents looking for their children
Buried among the rubble
Searching, searching, nothing found
Like being trapped in a big round bubble.

All the crumbled remains of Haiti
Nobody there to give them aid
Screaming, shouting, nothing worked
That earthquake had them slayed.

Jamie Stenning (13)
Humphrey Perkins High School, Barrow Upon Soar

Poetry

To write a poem
You require inspiration
Something to write a poem about
You require some creation.

After that it all depends
On how the poet is feeling
The entire mood of the poem depends
On what the poet finds appealing.

All their emotions written down on a page
But other things are needed also
Such as rhythm, rhyme and relevance
And a creative mind, more so.

Some things to be included are
Enjambment, alliteration and repetition
Metaphors and personification
Are needed in addition.

To write a poem is really easy
Write down your thoughts, feelings and desires
Or a poem can tell a story
Designed to frighten, mystify or inspire.

All poems are really beautiful
They last for years and years
A poem can be a most wonderful thing
Music to one's ears.

Samantha Vesty (13)
Humphrey Perkins High School, Barrow Upon Soar

The Maze

I feel no fear
For there is no one to hear
My footsteps whisper through the night
The darkness covers me and bars my sight.
But there is nowhere to go
The world has hidden all it has to show.
The rain falls down over me
Falling from the stars it seems
Through parting clouds descends new light
To all those darkened days I say goodnight.
I could never go back nor be the same
The passion to escape burns inside like a flame,
Nearing the exit I quicken my pace
For the first time I search this place
For a meaning, a whisper, or a clue.
Nothing is what I thought I knew
A smile lifts the darkened haze
I found the way out of this maze.

Sophie Nelson (13)
Humphrey Perkins High School, Barrow Upon Soar

Twenty20 World Cup

Twelve of the world's best cricket teams
Ready for the cup in the shortest games.

All the players had travelled far
Apart from the West Indies who sat at the bar.

An international debut for Afghanistan
But could they beat the holders, the legendary Pakistan?

England's first game was against the hosts
Whichever team won had planned to boast.

England had got 192 but because of the rain
The West Indies triumphed so England left with no gain.

But after this they pulled it together
They got to the final, they will remember this forever.

They pulled it off, thanks to Kieswetter
After all that doubt from the betters.

George Thompson (13)
Humphrey Perkins High School, Barrow Upon Soar

My Two Flying Wings

My two flying wings, you must fly
Don't give up, we must carry on -
You look invisible to everyone else
But I believe that you're real
So let's dare fly.
No need to jump on steps
I will just aim very high
And I know we will make it
To the other side.

Nobody put a hole in my wings
My two flying wings need to fly
Nobody steal my mirror
I'm not blind
Who dares show me right and wrong
I have already learned
Both of those lessons.
Last, don't breathe for me anybody
I can hold my own breath and that's how I control
Both of my two flying wings
To fly straight forward and high
By any means
That I may need.

Tatiana Lelo (17)
James Brindley School, Birmingham

Me

I feel so confused
I wish I could break free
I struggle so much to be me.

I lie in bed at night
Wishing that everything would be all right
I feel alone
All my hope is gone
Till I pick up the phone.

I wish I could break free
So I could be me
Every day feels like one
Nowadays I don't know what to do
I wish things could be different
But they aren't.

I wish I could break free
So I could just be me
Sometimes I cry myself to sleep
My life's empty, my heart feels tight
And nobody is doing anything to make it right
I wish I could be me
So I could just be free.

Ebony Danielle Melrose (17)
James Brindley School, Birmingham

The Christmas Day

Sleep-logged, unmoving, as if corpse-like
Parents slumber in their warm duvet landscape
Shortly to be awakened by their young
Children, elated by the happiness of the day
Leap and fly, soaring around the bed
The day has come and there's no stopping
As they beg. Grovelling, praying, pleading
For 'just one, Mummy!' eyes alight with wonder
Adults sigh as the day has just begun.

Glistening polished shoes stand on ceremony
On the chilling hardwood floor. For once
The children ready and dressed
Crumpled shirts hanging out, dresses not quite done up
The mother, impeccably attired
In an old, tired dressing gown and frizzy morning hair
In the kitchen already, preparing a tidy royal breakfast
Succulent crackling bacon seared to perfection
And fried eggs, rich and heavy. Their yolks, coagulated suns.

Preparation complete and a full family
All gather and encircle the tree, its leaves untouched by the falling snow
Emerald-green branches protecting its cargo's mystery
On the signal, youth dive. Eyes at bursting points. Smiles wide.
Rapid ripping of the wrapping paper unveils
Surprise after surprise. Glorious in array
Thanks all around as the Everest
Of gifts and goodies slowly depletes
Amongst the cackle of laughter and mumbles of joy
Carols of church-goers are barely heard.

There goes the oven. Around the table, they gather
Confetti, holly and snowflakes, the foliage decorating the table
A turkey, golden in its crown, jewelled with gems of gravy and seasoning
The necessary trimmings follow their monarch, complimenting its glory.

The court jesters, the crackers, bangs and pops, their intestinal-
streamers
Sail through the air. Their hearts of jokes and toys bring smiles to
faces
The ringing of crystal as the patriarch makes a speech
But to then swig back the glass unceremoniously
Accompanied by a resounding, 'Hick!'

An abandoned board game lies on the coffee table
Its companion, the television listings sleeps beside it
Its face graffitied by the circled Christmas movie
Grandparents snore on the collapsing sofa whilst the children are put
to work
In the kitchen loading and drying dishes
Mother still slaves though she hasn't stopped all day
She waits until it is her turn to relax
To sink into bed with a large coffee would be her present
With the snow swirling and dancing on the wind outside.

Rebecca Millar (16)
Leicester High School for Girls, Leicester

Surrender

A depressing room filled with mourning
She has gone, now my heart is torn
I surrender; I fall to my feet
She sucked my life just like a leech
Cold and bitter for my love
I surrender to above
Finished my journey, all over now
Not once been washed, in shame, my head down
Alas no more pain
Forget my new life, forever and plain
Before I leave I seat and bathe
And think about my incoming faith.

Simran Roshan (10)
Leicester High School for Girls, Leicester

Lady Lucifer

(A poem in the style of Carol Ann Duffy)

Living with him isn't what you'd think
Fire, excitement, burning passion
Heat danger, risk
No.
That's what I bought into
Sold my soul
Came down here
But no.

Saw him once, that was it
Dancing, capering,
laughing, cackling
He hypnotised me
thick black hair, bulging muscles
sparkling eyes, late night tussles
life in the fire
life on the edge
Life.

But what's a demon when he's at home?
Not a demon. An angel, fallen.
Walks in at night
Monster? Mean? Menace?
(Sits)
Man. Nothing more.

He'd phone Yahweh on a Saturday night
debated the finer points of life, death and politics.
Well if you get goodness and purity, then I get science.
he'd say.
Oh come on now it's only fair . . .
Diplomatic
Day-to-day
Dull!

I bore his child too, little girl
little kid, little tyke, little devil
Daughter of Satan, Witch.
He doted on her: loving.

Kind. The last straw
The cherry on the cake
Glacé is cold
Glamour is but skin deep.

They were wrong, those writers
Matthew, Mark, Luke, John
Milton
Wrong.

I hitched a lift with the boat man
I walked on the wilder side
I went searching for a man who's a devil
Leaving my 'devil' behind.

Hannah Bristow (17)
Leicester High School for Girls, Leicester

Colourful Rainbow

Rainbow, rainbow, so merry and bright
Each colour has a purpose and a light

Your array of colours so sparkly and fair
Magical dust sweeps through the air

I make a wish so my dreams come true
Pink, yellow, green and blue

When the sun goes away you hide too
I wait for another one of you.

Sania Akhtar-Hassan (10)
Leicester High School for Girls, Leicester

The Empty Bag

The empty bag
The story of my life
Like an unfinished painting
Or a blunt knife.

The empty bag
It's cold, weak and bare
Add the dust that rises up
Equals: unfair.

The empty bag
It seems to say it's really sad
As it seems to cry and whimper
I feel guilty, defeated and bad.

The empty bag
Though empty, once loved
Like a deserted ghost town
Like a shot-down dove.

Phoebe Love (11)
Leicester High School for Girls, Leicester

Mum

She is the one who soaks my tears like a cushion
And fills my sorrow with hope and joy.
Who guides me with her gentle hands
Her eyes full of dazzling hope
Her unwavering smile full of comfort and warmth
Who is charming and sweet
Sparkly rainbows open as she sits in the room
She is a gift from Heaven
If I could have chosen, I would have picked no other
That is why she is the most special part of my life
Who I will treasure forever.

Aditi Pant (11)
Leicester High School for Girls, Leicester

The Environment

Children playing, having fun
Running into sea, so clear and blue
Swimming far away, not coming back
With kites flying high in the sky
And the magic of the crashing waves
It's all so beautiful and content
They are excited to go in
What we have done
It's true we have polluted the sea
No more excitement for you and me.

Aerosols might harden your hair
But have you thought about the air?
What has it done to you?
Now it smells of poo
Shh, shh here, shh, shh there
And spray it everywhere
You need to lighten up
Like that empty can. Yuck!
The time has come, don't use up all your luck.

When I walk I look around
At the trees planted on the ground
All the leaves scattered
Different shades all battered
The next time I walked
I saw nothing
Because people chopped them down
Now you have learned my story
Think from this poem!

Anya Agnihotri (11)
Leicester High School for Girls, Leicester

Animals

Animals are cute and furry,
Tall or short, fat or skinny
Some have four legs, some have two
Some are soft and some are scaly
Pretty and beautiful
Some have good eyesight
Some are healthy, some have been abandoned
Some owners are kind, some are cruel
I love animals and now you do too!

Georgie Parker (11)
Leicester High School for Girls, Leicester

Love

I hold it true, whate'er befall
I feel it, when I sorrow most
Tis better to have loved and lost
Than never to have loved at all.

Verity Howell (11)
Leicester High School for Girls, Leicester

Intangible Rhythm

Intangible rhythm, unknowable melody
It. Doesn't. Make. Sense.
But neither does non-fiction.

Absorbant discordance
To. Your.
Shoebox of special memories
Ov.er. Your.
Pillow stained red with jealousy
Un.im.por.tant.
Your well-known secrets and hate affairs.

Forced love and beautiful hate
To.geth.er. Make.
Whatever you are told to see.

You were born into passive violence,
Un.fair.
Your horseshoe doesn't fix it
Un.der. There.
Heard tears from on a broken chair,
Why. Can't. You. See.
Yourself behind the make-up's light.

Intangible rhythm, unknowable melody,
You. Haven't. Seen. Sense.
If you're still following this hypocrisy.

Henry Bennison (16)
Lincoln Minster School, Lincoln

Sad Pictures And Happy Endings

It's a sad picture
Another blow hits you
My car drives off
You're left behind
Standing by your house
Again.

We're not together much
I never see you now
It's the same every week
Our time is sacrificed
Because I'm busy
Again.

I love you, but how to show it?
I used to know how
Now I let you down
And you're just waiting
Always there, while I'm busy
Again.

You always said it'd get worse before it got better
I never believed you, now I do
But you seem to forget it will get better
You can have my time once more
You can feel safe and secure
Just like once before.

Ten years on . . .
What did I tell you?
It got better after it got worse
I'm a busy, stressed teenager no more
No homework, no one telling me what to do
And a ring on my finger which binds me to you.

Beth Higgins (14)
Newport Girls' High School, Newport

Goldilocks And The Three Bears

Goldilocks, the little brute
Had an eye for finding loot
And so it came to be that she
Broke in the house of the bears three.

Skipping on, the vile brat
Stepped inside and promptly spat.
The glint vanished from her grey eyes;
The room was bare, but for some flies.

'Drat!' she cried, then smiled and said:
'Then I'll take their food instead!'
For in the next room, porridge stood
In three big bowls (they smelled quite good!)

One mouthful later - 'Ow!' she cried;
'These dumb bears can't cook,' she sighed.
The first bowl scalded her tongue red -
The next two left her tastebuds dead!

In the next room she found chairs -
Two large, one small, built for bears.
She tried the smallest chair out first,
But under her great weight, it burst!

'Oh poor me!' the cockroach moaned.
'I must find a bed!' she groaned.
But then, what she failed to foresee,
In came the bears, one, two and three.

With a twisted smile said she:
'Sorry guys, but, wel, you see . . .
I'm still peckish, so say your prayers!'
And then she gobbled up the bears.

Tabitha Heeley (14)
Newport Girls' High School, Newport

Death In The Trenches

I'm miles away
But you'll always stay
Right there in my heart
Where you were from the start
I miss you so dearly
And I'm not thinking clearly
I'm depressed
I'm obsessed
Because I am dirty
And have been for thirty
Days and nights
There are no lights
In the rooms where we sleep
Laugh, write and weep
So it's always dark
That's why there is a boot mark
On this letter that I'm jotting
But wait now, I'm spotting
The Germans
Got my gun
Won't be fun
I might not come back
In which case Sergeant Black
Will post this to you
And I hope you read it through
I want to be free
Lots of love, Lee.

Jenny Smith (13)
Newport Girls' High School, Newport

Dear Mummy . . .

Dear Mummy
I don't know what to say
I wish I had those 10 minutes back
Before I went to play.

You told me not to speak to those
I had not met before
You told me they were nasty
They'd throw me to the floor.

So when I saw that man
Who carried those red sweets
I immediately walked by fast
And didn't even speak.

He grabbed me by my arm
And whispered in my ear,
I wriggled and I squirmed, thinking,
There's no one to help me here.

He hit me with his fist
And took me in his arms
He didn't even care
That I was bleeding from my palms.

Ten minutes was all it took
Though my death was long and slow
You soon came to look for me
I couldn't tell you I was dead though.

Emma Higgins (14)
Newport Girls' High School, Newport

One Small Step for Man, One Giant Leap For Mankind

1st July 1926
A boy set about with a handful of sticks
He moulded and folded, twisted and stuck
Creating the space rocket, so that people could look
At the brilliant array of twinkling stars
And could one day visit the planet Mars!

3rd October 1937
A man set about to reach the boundaries of Heaven
He ordered and shouted, whipped and scold
Watching the poor, famished prisoners, which he controlled
Create the V2 rocket right under his nose
So that Adolf Hitler could bring England to blows.

9th August 1941
A man was on the run from the deeds he had done
He ran and sprinted, hurtled and dashed
To save being caught for the lives he had smashed
The Americans came, and saw what he had made
And helped sort out the lives of so many needing aid.

20th July 1969
A man travelled into space on the rocket design
He clapped and smiled, rejoiced and cheered
And overcame all the difficulties which he had feared
Going down in history as the man who allowed
For a moment that man could be unbelievably proud.

Naomi Gulliver (14)
Newport Girls' High School, Newport

Please Don't Go

Please don't you worry
Please don't be sad
Whatever is happening
Can't be that bad.

Think about how lucky
You really are
Don't mess with my head
Don't take it that far.

Don't say stupid things
Don't try to get out
You would be so missed
Without a doubt.

I don't want you to go
Please try to live on
Already I'm dreading
The day you are gone
Forever.

Because when you end it
When you pull the plug
There's no coming out
Of the grave that you dug.

Ellie Bryan (14)
Newport Girls' High School, Newport

Saving The Abandoned

Thousands of small animals
Locked up in a shed
Nothing left to eat
A horrible life they have led.

No way to get out
Their fur is ridden with fleas
The light from the window gets blocked
Finally, somebody sees.

The RSPCA come
And break down the door
Take them all away
The dirty cages are left on the floor.

The man that owned the shed
Gets fined and sent to court
He cannot keep animals again
And lost the battle that he fought.

It is a sad story
Some had to be put down
But the rest are perky animals
Waiting for their home to be found.

Jen Clarke (14)
Newport Girls' High School, Newport

I Could . . . But I'm Not

I'm gonna be a blonde
So that we can bond
Short, pink, pretty skirt
I ain't gonna mess in dirt.

I'll be a red-head
Just to get in your bed
Bright and bubbly to make my mark
Or maybe you want seductive and dark?

If I dye my hair black
Would you cut me some slack?
Yeah, if they stare
Shall I say it's a dare?

I could be brunette
You'd notice me then, I bet
We remember: that's what they say
But I don't wanna last just one day.

But I'm not . . . I'm me
What you get, is what you see
Course, your opinion's fair
But really? I don't care.

Lucie Price (14)
Newport Girls' High School, Newport

You Broke Her Heart

We see her sitting there all alone
Shaking, to the very bone
We all tried, yes we really did
But you see, she's no longer a kid.

Her heart was broken in two
Our best friend was hurt because of you
You don't realise what you've done
Last night we found her with a gun.

You hurt her in so many ways
And now her life is so grey
She doesn't even cry
We don't even hear a sigh.

She cries about the girl at your arm
The one you gained with your false suave charm
Our best friend is hurt because of you
You broke her heart into two.

Dimple Mistry (14)
Newport Girls' High School, Newport

Love Is . . .

Love is . . .
The rising sun within my heart,
My senses pierced by Cupid's dart,
Like reflections of my dream-filled nights.
Stormy water; dazzling bright.

Love is . . .
A torturous pit of burning emotion,
Blind, self-sacrificing: blinkered devotion,
Like nightmares eating up my sleep,
My sanity not mine to keep.

Love is . . .
The waves that crash against the shore,
Drenching my soul, washing it pure,
A rope of roses, red and strong,
Never to be broken, infinitely long.

Kayleigh Woodhouse (14)
Newport Girls' High School, Newport

Love

Love, an endeavour most noble and true,
contrary to the fleeting pleasures;
the fruit with which the spindled tree of lust
doth entice poor misled and hungry pilgrims -
we hath strayed so far.
This fruit; soft, plump, ripe - to the eye and hand alike,
tempts sweet love-seeking pilgrims from their sweet love-seeking paths,
by way of giving cause to them to think they are misconstrued in cause
thus their voyage for that fleece of gold
yon through and past this beating sea, is fruitless.
Damn that tree, with illusions coy,
and fruit, whom at first, to the tongue buds sweet,
flowers' bitter gall that doth spurn and humour any fallacial sweet.
Hearty reason from the mist restored,
doth make the eyes turn shrewd at such carnal haste,
as hindsight th'abacus of the blind man he,
thus foresight that of the wise man he.
But wise's only blind that hath apparatus well used,
thus no more this path of love abused.
This path of love God-patronned in its name,
hath like the dagger's edge - a wayside yard
above which church doth stand and spires point,
in misfortun'd souls doth lay at rest - and mourn
the unconcluded channel once besailed - with yearning eyes.
But 'Love from Love; the cure tis in the phrased,
thus thy discourse - be sure till be erased . . .
give all thyself unto thy fellow he,
and in return thy treasure wished by thee.

Christian Luke Da'Costa (16)
Ninestiles School, Acocks Green

I Only Want You

The tides are finally starting to change
It's a lot better with you by my side
I can't speak to you; you are out of range
I know you're doing this just for the ride.

My love is still warm, but yours has gone cold
You obviously don't want us to be
We'll be together until you grow old
I don't understand why you don't want me.

You're annoying, always changing your mind
You don't want to do this? Oh well, too late
You were always nasty, when I was kind
All I want is you, only you Katie

You made a promise which you just can't keep
It's all your fault that I can't get to sleep.

Andrew Parry (16)
Ninestiles School, Acocks Green

To My Beloved

Loving you when it became an option
I didn't fall but stood with one foot on the ground
And the other in the air, could one say part of me was living in a fantasy?
And the other brought back to reality when complications arose outside
or even sometimes within this suspicious relationship.
Youth at this time lacks neither insecurity nor immaturity
but tomorrow will create chaos for the question of you being faithful
and honest will come into play.
Amorous this feeling
left behind words we could never find to explain ourselves
to say that the love is beyond the heart
reaches for thoughts, borrows them
and soon they become words we forget to say.
Awareness of the fact that you could move on haunts me every day
just the thought of you being far away.
I want your love to reflect God's heart for me of never-ending love
but never losing hope.
You always come back
I think some days I have all the pieces to the puzzle entitled 'our relationship'
but always there is no way to connect it
for when you're close you are what I want I know
but confusion is then brought on by arguments so small
but, being the sweetest sin
your love sometimes leaves me in a state of apathy
with no aplomb
but as abysmal as it is to say this I will, I want to run
but only far enough to make you miss me.

Nicolette Hibbert (18)
Northampton College, Northampton

This Is Me

I might not drink or smoke
It doesn't mean I'm a loser
Just because I don't party all night
Doesn't mean I have no life
I might not get into trouble all the time
Doesn't make me a *saddo*
Just because I'm not skinny
Doesn't make me fat
I might not have ever had a boyfriend
Doesn't make me a sore sight
Just because I'm Christian
Doesn't make me a Bible-basher
I might like kiddie stuff
But it doesn't make me a baby
Just because I wanna do well in school
Doesn't make me a geek

This is me
And this is how I shall always be
The good, the bad and the ugly
If you like me or not
I don't mind
'Cause this is me
And you can't change that.

Jo Pilkington (14)
St George's Academy, Sleaford

The World We Live In

God make us equal, no one's better than anyone, but people beg to differ.
People carry knives for protection and people carry them to hurt people
But carry a knife and end a life.
Some with guns, people think they're cool and fun
But they're not, they are made to kill
People in gangs carry both which is dumb
Because if you get caught, you will go to prison
Which is not nice when you go down for five to life.

Dealing or taking drugs is a mug's game
Pills, powders, potions are not good
People take them to look cool
But when they're addicted, living in an alleyway
Or on the streets or going mentally insane
Or dying, they don't look cool then, do they?
God must be looking down on them, like 24-hour surveillance
Thinking they have just wasted their lives, either in prison or drugged up.
But sometimes they could have a gang war and people get shot
Or stabbed, for what?
All because they live in a different area code, that's stupid
So I wonder what God thinks about the world we live in?

Charlie Strachan (13)
St George's Academy, Sleaford

Nature

Trees stand tall and proud reaching for the sunlight
Big strong stags having a very dangerous fight
Bears waiting for the fish, ha, ha, they wish
Bees fly from flower to flower
There is often a very heavy shower
Cuckoos stealing other birds' eggs, oh what a crime
Chicks leaving the nest for the very first time
Wild flowers grow in the tall green grass
Spiderwebs glisten like brand new glass
Leaves fall down on the hard ground
Not making a single sound
Snow drifts down covering the land in white
Oh what a sight
Rivers flow fast and slow in the sun
It gives a beautiful glow.

Chloe Blades (14)
St George's Academy, Sleaford

Life

If life was easy, no troubles, no tears
If life was calm, no pain, no fears
But we have all had our trouble and strife
We have to admit it is the pattern of life.

Life was better back in the day
Being with friends just to play
No idea of money or wealth
Only worry was our family's life.

People were alive who are gone today
Wish we could see them but there is no way
But we meet new friends
All good things come to an end.

There is nothing certain apart from death
And that always is at the end.

Liam Conroy (14)
St Thomas Aquinas Catholic School, Kings Norton

Boom! Boom! Boom!

Boom! Boom! Boom!
His heart
Beating like it was about to
Shout out
Like a bullet
Being triggered out of a loaded
AK47 gun.

Bang!
His head stopped
With shock
Looking in the black sky
He froze with a gulp
His eyes widening.

He looked ahead
A soft thump to the ground
Everywhere was silent
His hands shaking with fear.

He took a long deep breath
Looked down and blinked twice
Seeing a body lying across the floor
Dead!

He rubbed his eyes
To check again
To see if what he saw was real
But nothing, that same loaded
AK47 gun
Now unloaded right by his feet.

He stood there in amazement
Thinking to himself.
I'm not dead
Crying with happiness
Knowing he killed
His enemy and that he has now
Survived!

Danea Campbell (14)
St Thomas Aquinas Catholic School, Kings Norton

If

(Inspired by Rudyard Kipling's 'If')

If you can look at yourself and smile
And never get the feeling of denial
If you can walk with your head held high
And never let out a doubtful sigh
If you can be your own person
And not hide behind a curtain
If you're the person people rely on
Just make sure you have someone to fall upon
If you like to watch television
But not make that your only vision
If you can work hard in your GCSEs
And aim for those A, B or Cs
If you can open your heart to everyone
And maybe some day find your special someone
If you dream about fairy tales and love
But know it won't just fall from above
If you can keep secrets to yourself
And not let them run out of your mouth
If you like to look good and not get vain
Then people won't think you're a pain
If you can live your life to the full
And not let your face look dull
If you can fantasise over gorgeous celebrities
But know hard work is your expertise
If you cannot get involved in all the drama
Because it is all a load of palaver
If you have all of these qualities
Then you have endless possibilities
Your life will be whatever you make it
And you will never end up in the pit.

Hannah Doyle (14)
St Thomas Aquinas Catholic School, Kings Norton

I Must Pay

I love you . . .
I really do
For all of the things
You say and you do
Alas there's one catch
I really have to say
Love me you do not
So now I must pay . . .

I must pay for your eyes
So beautifully blue
I must pay for your smile
So beautiful too
I must pay for my feelings
Which burden me so
With love and joy
Sadness and sorrow.

I must pay for the people
Who've gone through this too
I must pay for how
They all pulled through
I must pay for everything
Yet nothing at all
I must pay for my sins
That burn me like gall.

I must pay for the way
I've treated my friends
How cold I have been
Yet not making amends.

Kavan Green (13)
St Thomas Aquinas Catholic School, Kings Norton

Will You My Boy?

Who's for the battle?
Are you my boy?
Who'll grab victory?
Will you my boy?
Don't be afraid
it's just like a game
But who'll stand clear and bite his thumbs
Will you my boy?

Who's keen on saving lives?
And means to show his grit?
Are you my boy?
Who'll earn his country's thanks?
Who'll stand a coward?
Will you my boy?

Whose guns will echo from the distance?
Screams and cries of people's terrors
Will you my boy?
Saving children who are
Wandering in this poverty-stricken land
Will you help peace rise on this Earth?

Won't back down
Long to charge and shoot
Will you my boy?
Who'll watch the bullets whiz past
Will you my boy?

Alice McIntosh (14)
St Thomas Aquinas Catholic School, Kings Norton

I Believe In You

(Inspired by Rudyard Kipling's 'If')

If you can be oh so wise
Or be someone else just to disguise

If you have an achievement in life, a goal
Just try your best and believe in your soul

If you try but fail, don't lose your head
Just don't give up, try instead

If you find that special one
Who you shall always call upon
Hold them dearly with all your might
And care for them, day and night

If you get a job and succeed in life
Do not wreck it with trouble and strife

In life if you have qualifications
You can get a job and go on vacation

If you are willing in life which you are
Eventually in life you could become a star

And all those years that will pass by
You'll be wondering how time flies

So you endeavour in life to succeed
I think you could be a proper *human being*!

Daniel Moore (14)
St Thomas Aquinas Catholic School, Kings Norton

Hope

It's morning now, the night has passed
My friend and I survived the blast
We walked along the damaged street
Slates from roofs beneath our feet
As we go through this devastation
It takes more than bombs to crush this nation.

Rebecca Dunbar (14)
St Thomas Aquinas Catholic School, Kings Norton

The Twin Towers

Remember me?
I was in a beautiful city with many decorations
I had a friend by my side
I was very bold and never thought of anyone hurting me
For years everyone praised me
As I stood proudly

It was a peaceful day
And everything was normal
I towered over the familiar faces
Staring back at me in awe
As I stood prouder than ever

Suddenly a great ball of fire came upon me
'Ouch,' I said but everyone was busy
Soon I burned into a flame fire
I looked for my friend
But he was gone too

Years have passed by
Yet I'm still remembered
Each year on September 11th, families gather
They stare up at where I once stood in sorrow
For now I am not so proud.

Hannah Sweeney (14)
St Thomas Aquinas Catholic School, Kings Norton

Ambition

Ambition drives everyone
It takes control of you
You simply can't resist ambition
It takes you to your goal
It keeps you going to the very end
You need it through life
As you strive to achieve through obstacles
And uncover the hidden mysteries of ambition.

Jordan Pinnock-Miller (14)
St Thomas Aquinas Catholic School, Kings Norton

Friendship

Friendship, what does it mean to me?
Doesn't matter if it's a he or a she
Loyal, loveable, caring and understanding
It is really baffling.

Friendship, is like a day in May
Laughing, singing, crying all day
The ones who I personally chose
Who would stick by me really close.

Friendship, is when you tell someone everything
Who you tell a secret or just anything
They are the people who help you when you're down
Whenever you laugh, cry, smile or frown.

Friendship, is something to treasure
But the love between them is never measured
Good friends are hard to find
Not to see it you must be blind.

I love my friends' sarcasm and humour
Even if they spread a fake rumour
One in a million is what my friends are
To find others better, you have to go far.

Charmaine Espinoza (14)
St Thomas Aquinas Catholic School, Kings Norton

War

War is terrible, is sad, full of death
Men die and many are lost to the trenches
Trenches are full of corpses and injured
Injured or dying, all alone in pain
Living and screaming in horror at life
The dead are silent, cold, in death's hard grip
The survivors scream in hospital beds
The civilians wonder why I live
War is terrible, is sad, full of death.

John Raven (14)
St Thomas Aquinas Catholic School, Kings Norton

The Death Game

The sound of guns echoed in my ears
As I was walking through the field of death
Where many lay with closed eyes
Sorrow and sadness filled my heart
I wondered why I was standing there
And soon I realised, it was not a game.

A bomb blew in front of me
A gunshot behind me
Men died beside me
I had a feeling inside me
It said, *why am I here?*

Am I a hero or a coward?
Should I run to save my life
Or should I die for my country
Or should I leave in disappointment?

A bomb blew in front of me
A gunshot behind me
Men died beside me
I had a feeling inside me
It said, *why am I here?*

Cleopatra Madziwa (13)
St Thomas Aquinas Catholic School, Kings Norton

Thought

School can be boring sometimes you know
We all know you'd rather be at home watching a TV show.
But if you put some thought
Into what you're being taught
Then maybe, just maybe
Depending on the economy
You might just do well in this life.

Declan Reville (14)
St Thomas Aquinas Catholic School, Kings Norton

If
(Inspired by Rudyard Kipling's 'If')

If you can admit your fears
And face your troubles
Down four pints of beer
And shave your stubble

If you can fight till the end
And battle for the ones that you love
If your back will bend
To bring peace like a dove

If you can go through life with no regrets
And not be ashamed of who you are
If you get put down and still show respect
And love them who have left you scarred

If you battle away
For those who are weak
If you can play
Without having to cheat

Then you are truly a man my friend
The biggest opportunities are around the bend.

Matthew Georgiou (14)
St Thomas Aquinas Catholic School, Kings Norton

Dreams

Dream as you live, live your dreams
If you do you're sure to succeed
Make sure no one gets in your way
Set your goals in life, strive to achieve
Do your very best and get As, Bs or Cs
See the sights, visit them all
And I can assure you you'll have a ball
As time goes by, trust me, it flies
Do what you can, the limit is the skies
We're all living on borrowed time.

Tre'Rail Peters (13)
St Thomas Aquinas Catholic School, Kings Norton

Wars!

There have been three wars in 100 years
Pray to God that they're all OK
Some of us have realised our worst fears
Even though they risk their lives, it isn't the best of pay!

In 1914, we started a war
And in 1918 it was the end
It left us all quite poor
Leaving the stock market on a downward bend
But all in all, we won the war!

Twenty-one years later, the second world war had started
It was Britain and France against the Germans
At the end of the war, some of Germany was parted
In 1945 the war had ended, unlike the first war we were not poor
And again we had won the war!

Now in 2010 another war is going on
The war is in Afghanistan
The American and the British are fighting all the Taliban
Can we win the war? I hope we can!

Luke Kiely (14)
St Thomas Aquinas Catholic School, Kings Norton

If

(Inspired by Rudyard Kipling's 'If')

If you can give and share what's yours in life
And in your lifetime get a husband or wife
If you can keep a well-earned job
And not get caught up in a group of mobs
If secrets are told, don't tell any other
As it's just as bad as cheating on your lover
If you can walk with your head held high
And never in your life deal in lies
You'll become the person you want to be
As long as you're true and trust me!

Courtney Burley (13)
St Thomas Aquinas Catholic School, Kings Norton

If

(Inspired by Rudyard Kipling's 'If')

If you can keep your temper when people hurt you
Or can keep calm in a situation
If you can pass your driving test in one go
Or play a sport and pass the ball to and fro
If you can own a pet to love and care about
Or talk to someone who annoys you and do not shout.

If you can find a woman who's loving and kind
But make sure she's clever in the mind
If you can get a good job with decent pay
Or stand up in a crowd and speak your beliefs
Or walk through a forest and not step on a leaf.

If you can work your hardest and don't complain
Or go by yourself on the midnight train
Or as an old man look in a mirror and look the same
If you can be generous and not take credit for what you've done
And once more you'll be a man my son.

Luke Farrell (14)
St Thomas Aquinas Catholic School, Kings Norton

If

(Inspired by Rudyard Kipling's 'If')

If you can try your best in school
And never give up, even if you fall
If you can hear rumours about you
But not tell lies about them too
If you can be told a secret
And not whisper a word
If you cannot be over-confident
But still be heard
If you can do all of the things
I have said
Then you will have a bright future ahead.

Claire Walsh (14)
St Thomas Aquinas Catholic School, Kings Norton

Are You . . . You?

Do you act differently around the other lot?
Do you cover yourself up to be someone you're not?
How will people know who you really are?
Are you that one who goes a bit too far?
Don't wear a mask and look false
You're insecure and that's all you can take.

Just take the time to stop and think
Are you . . . you?

Do you have that friend who talks behind your back?
Are you the one who's lost in the pack?
Do you have that person who laughs and calls you names?
Do they know that it pains?
Now let's make it clear and get things straight
Go! You can do it and take the leap of faith!

Just take the time to stop and think
Are you . . . you?

Molly McDonald (13)
St Thomas Aquinas Catholic School, Kings Norton

If

(Inspired by Rudyard Kipling's 'If')

If you can always try your best
And always aim to succeed
If you can go it alone, fly the nest
And help all those in need
If you can admit when you are wrong
And forgive when others are too
If you can get through the day, short or long
And live a life that's not just about you
If you can make the best of a bad situation
And use wisely all of your time
If you can be happy in your occupation
Then you'll be just fine!

Jodie Carey (14)
St Thomas Aquinas Catholic School, Kings Norton

Vote For Me!

Election day is coming,
Oh what am I to do?
Advertise? Legalise?
Make a brand of shoe?

Take out the competition!
Have a live debate!
Organise petitions,
Our country's in a state!

I'll publish all my speeches.
Change the party's point of view,
They'll cling to me like leeches!
I'll count on your vote too!

The papers make me look bad,
What can I do for them?
I'll strive my best to win . . .
Election 2010!

Josh Gannon (14)
St Thomas Aquinas Catholic School, Kings Norton

Silent Warfare

Shh, what's that?
He looks left
Looks right
Up
But not down
Big mistake
He's underneath
The enemy goes for the melee
The enemy misses
He panics and empties his whole clip
From his silenced assault rifle
'The enemy' is dead.

Joel Healy (14)
St Thomas Aquinas Catholic School, Kings Norton

Summer

Watching the sky on a summer's day
Listening to the birds chirping away
There's a smell of cut grass in the air
And sounds of kids screaming at the fair
At the beach in the sun
Or in the garden having fun
The summer has just begun!

Having a barbecue with my friends
Hoping this weather never ends
Playing around in the pool
While Dad shows off and thinks he's cool
Mom sunbathes and uses her fan
In the sun for hours, getting a tan
That was my summer
It was so much fun
But now I'm upset that it's all done.

Ellen Herbert (13)
St Thomas Aquinas Catholic School, Kings Norton

Love

The amazing eyes
I do get lost in those eyes
His sense of humour
It makes me cry from laughter.

When he looks at me
He stuns me into silence
When he smiles at me
Butterflies quickly appear.

In times like these
I remember I love you.

Paige Ridley (14)
St Thomas Aquinas Catholic School, Kings Norton

Down The Blues

Keep right on, the Blues fans sing
As Seb Larsson springs down the wing
Looking for someone who is open
Pass, he shoots, as the defence is broken
The Blues are up one goal to nil
'C'mon Villa,' says Villa fan Bill.

Agbonlahor sprints avoiding the players
'Stop him!' Johnson is heard from the mayor's
He takes the shot, quick like a dart
Only to be saved, the number one, Joe Hart
Joe Hart kicks the ball high up in the ground
To be picked up by Lee Bowyer and look around
He goes to take a shot, all power behind the ball
When the ball is kicked, breaks through the defender's wall
It's aiming for top right hoping for the best
It's in, we are the best, better than the rest.

Liam Connolly (14)
St Thomas Aquinas Catholic School, Kings Norton

Ireland - Haiku

Beautiful Ireland
Fresh green grass all around us
The country I love.

Adam McKinley (14)
St Thomas Aquinas Catholic School, Kings Norton

Death

The time will come
When death will arise to greet you
At your own door, for your own soul
At each will be petrified to see one another.

And when it says, 'Come let's go.'
You will then again become the soul
That you were before coming to this world
You will try to capture all your laughter
As you go out through your door into the sparkling blue sky.

Doors will open, angels will sing for you to enter
For once you'll be in a wonderful, peaceful and heavenly world
You will once again rest in peace
As you will take down the heavenly showers
Death, you'll say, is not as bad as it seems.

Hafsa Rehman (13)
St Thomas Aquinas Catholic School, Kings Norton

The Birds

As I look outside my window high
I see a mother bird passing by
She settles down into her nest
And ruffles the feathers on her chest
To my surprise I see two white eggs
Then out pop two little legs
A head, a beak and four big eyes
The mother bird then says her goodbyes
She flies away from her humble nest
With the other birds heading west
I go outside and take a peek
At the little birds so small and weak
But don't worry birds, I'm here for you
To help you through this world so new.

Megan Cave & Aliji Ntima Garvis (12)
Sheffield High School, Sheffield

The Ballad Of Titanic

15th of April 1912
Two sixteen in the morn
Vast calamities struck a ship
Great disasters were born.

The huge ship was named Titanic
This boat had not one flaw
'Twas said to be unsinkable
Everyone stood in awe.

Now here's the tale of young lovers
Jack and Rose were their names
But Rose was to wed Cal Hockley
And Cal does not play games.

Dear Jack and Rose were forbidden
Even though they were pure
At first they mistook love for hate
They're perfect - that is sure.

Cal's invading spy had found them
Dancing with lower class
Cal could do nothing to stop it
He hoped that it would pass.

But sadly no, their love was strong
More so than any - ever
They were bound by their affections
Much, they did endeavour.

Then the time came, the sinking time
The time of much mourning
The stern rose up into the air
With not enough warning.

Screaming filled the air around Rose
Time - she wished she had more
So she searched for beloved Jack
Whilst looking for the shore.

Upon finding her freezing love
Whom she would not let go
Though dead, she still held his cold hand
Then let him drift below.

Jack was now dead, but Rose was alive
One brave lifeboat came back
But Rose did have one huge regret
That is not saving Jack.

Titanic would not sail again
Lost forever at sea
How do you think I knew all this?
Rose was, in fact, just me.

Jennyfer Reid (13)
Sheffield High School, Sheffield

The Haunted Footsteps

There is total silence
I lie completely still
My heart is racing
My breath penetrates the calm.

I lie completely still
The footsteps edge closer
My breath penetrates the calm
I close my eyes in case his face appears.

The footsteps edge closer
I get ready to scream
I close my eyes in case his face appears
No sound, but my breath penetrates the calm.

I get ready to scream
The moonlight shines on his face
No sound, but my breath penetrates the calm
Until there is chaos.

The moonlight shines on his face
My heart is racing
Until there is chaos
Then there is total silence.

Maddy Darling (12)
Sheffield High School, Sheffield

Dunblane Massacre - Sophie North

A hand print was all he had left
Printed against the glass
Her small hands were a memory
And the death of a class

Sophie North, just a little girl
Daddy won't clean the mark
Because that is all he has left
After her death so dark

Thomas Hamilton, who was he?
A man she didn't know
Armed, walked quickly into her class
Killed her brutally so

Standing by the dead and the dying
He showed no sympathy
It's called The Dunblane Massacre
Causing them misery

Miss Gwen Mayor was their hero
Died protecting children
Shielding the youngsters from gunfire
But still the man killed them

He was no man, nor ever was
He made his way across
Loading his guns with his ammo
To make another loss

As he ran towards them
They quickly took cover
As the angels looked down saying
He can't kill another

And yet he tried to do his worst
But what was done was done
Sophie was lying in cold blood
But Thomas hadn't won

All the pupils heard was silence
After the last gunshot
The killer Thomas Watt Hamilton
Will never be forgot

On Friday the 13th March
Sixteen young children died
Thomas Hamilton shot himself
And everybody cried

Sophie North, just a little girl
Daddy won't clean the mark
New laws were enforced to ban guns
After her death so dark.

Tayla Shelley (14)
Sheffield High School, Sheffield

Outer Space

Beautiful planets spinning in outer space
My eyes light up with wonder as I see their grace
Mercury, Venus, Earth, Mars, Jupiter, Saturn and Neptune
These are the planets in our solar system
They rotate round the sun, but they never do run.

My friends say I am a fool to think that the planets are cool
But I ignore them, they are mean
They don't know that I dream
The planets give me joy
And I don't want them to go away.

The sun is our source of light, it makes us very bright
Planet Earth is where we live, and it will never be at ease
This is where we will always be, we will never deceive it.

Mars is one of the planets
It is a red, fiery ball of hot gas
But I have never visited it, nor will I ever see it
Maybe I might if I become a scientist and explore it carefully.

Neptune is one of the planets
It is a cold, watery, blue ball
I don't want to visit, for it will probably freeze me.

Rhea Jain (12)
Sheffield High School, Sheffield

My Haiti Ballad

There was a tremendous earthquake
In Haiti this took place
A deep and tear-bringing story
A sad and moving case

One minute all was well and safe
The children played around
The dusty ground shook beneath them
Oh, what a deafening sound.

Houses brought down in mere minutes
Bodies under rubble
This moving thing happened so fast
Causing so much trouble

People screaming, crying on streets
Their children lost to find
Blood smeared on their broken faces
Lost in their worried minds

Mothers keep on sobbing deeply
They don't know what to do
Their babies gone for evermore
They barely have a clue

Children crying for their mothers
While vans drive slowly by
No one takes notice of them
Nobody even tries

These vans never have time to stop
No matter what they see
For beneath the thick, dark rubble
There are people to free

A few days passed before help came
People started to hope
That help would come in large amounts
So that the country coped

People flew in helicopters
Bringing water and food
Charities donated money
Helping lighten the mood

Slowly things began to rebuild
Children began to smile
Streets were cleared and rubble lifted
Hopefully for a while.

Francesca Diiasio (13)
Sheffield High School, Sheffield

Boy Stabs Younger Sibling

He looked out of his large window
To hear the doorbell ring
He looked down to the cracked doorstep
Then dropped his father's ring.

Tears rolled down from his red eyes
Bloodshot tears of shame
Blood on his hands and on the wall
But fame was not his game.

Dragging his sibling through dark Hell
The knife fell from his chest
He ripped off the red, bloody shirt
To find a bleeding breast.

The tale never made it on set
For the football coach sacked
Nobody heard of the story
Of the blade in the back.

Nobody ever found out why
A life ended this way
The oldest sibling locked in Hell
Hearing his brother's wail.

Did his brother ever feel bad
That he made an error?
Nobody read in the paper
Of this awful terror.

Ellie Needham (13)
Sheffield High School, Sheffield

Wave Of Sorrow

Her little soft hand encased in mine
I am distracted by her smile
My sweet darling playing in the sand
Just to watch makes my life worthwhile.

I watched as the sea was sucked back
And suddenly it went silent
It was like the calm before a storm
The normal sea was more violent.

But then a wave crashed down on the beach
With force that knocked me off my feet
The wave's huge strength swept me away
Carried me through my village street.

I was bashed and hit by cars and doors
Getting sucked under the water
My battered body almost gave in
But then I thought of my daughter.

With all my strength I clung to a tree
Willing myself to not let go
Hearing the scared screams of my friends
Praying for the water to slow.

The village I had known for so long
Flooded streets and houses destroyed
The wave took everything in its way
And left the people unemployed.

Everyone searched for their lost loved ones
Most of them would never return
But still they all kept waiting, hoping
I knew that most would never learn.

For days and days I just looked for her
Every time I heard footsteps I turned
I always saw her face in every child
She was gone but still I yearned.

If only God could rewind the past
With the wave that took her away
And give me back my dear baby
Because with her I died that day.

Her little soft hand encased in mine
I am distracted by her smile
My sweet darling playing in the sand
Without her my life's not worthwhile.

Shani Gill (12)
Sheffield High School, Sheffield

Somewhere In My Mind

There's a light glowing
Shining on my back
I don't believe it
I can't believe it

Shining on my back
I've been in the darkness too long
I can't believe it
This can't be possible

I've been in the darkness too long
My feelings have been numbed
This can't be possible
But it is

My feelings have been numbed
It can't be happiness
But it is
I can hear laughter somewhere in my mind

It can't be happiness
I'm scared
I'm shaking
I take a step

I'm scared
But I'm still brave
I take another step
There's a light glowing.

Lois Rands (13)
Sheffield High School, Sheffield

They Took What Was Left Of His Childhood

He had walked to the neighbouring village
For food to feed his hungry family.
Whilst he was away the soldiers came;
Shot them all dead,
Had them lined up,
In front of their houses;
And killed them all, or nearly all,
Leaving just one.

Alone he walked back into his lifeless village.
He knew before he even arrived at his house,
There was something about the quiet,
Not even the clicking of insects
Or the singing of birds,
As if in sympathy they remained silent.

Only fourteen years old when he found them,
All on the floor
Except his mother
Curled up, crouching motionless against the wall.
She couldn't speak
She couldn't move
She could only stare into space,
Without even a solitary tear
Trickling down her pale cheek.

He knelt down beside her,
Putting down the bundle of food,
Enough for a whole family;
And his battered football
That he had been given by his brothers.

He knew that she wished she were dead
But they knew it would hurt more to leave her alive
And when all humanity had left the humiliated retreating army
Their acts of atrocity were now the measure of their achievements.

They took money
They took valuables
They took life

They took any satisfaction that they could
From their victors

And in a moment of hatred
They took what was left of his childhood.

Natalia Hackett (13)
Sheffield High School, Sheffield

Star-Spangled Dream

The silver moon shines bright in the velvet sky
I look up, I see graceful owls fly
I lay down quiet, calm, still
Staring into the night for as long as I will.
The stars everywhere it's like artwork not a mess
I could wear it, my very own star-spangled dress.
The night is my refuge in times of trouble
My knight in shining armour, my very own bubble
To protect me and if there is anything scary like thunder
I've got my blue starry blanket to hide under
In a twisted light it seems quite frightening
Not so protective or enlightening
It seems to have lost its peaceful charm
It isn't quiet, still or calm.

The owls are scary, the night's ready to pounce
I don't think I even have an ounce
Of courage and strength to fight and banish it away
To the deepest corner of the Earth, that's where it will stay
Now I need my dreams to whisk me away
To comfort me and wash my fears away . . .
I am awake now and look, over there
The sun's light is shining over everyone, with lots to spare
The ball of fire, it brings the day
And banishes the spooky night away
As we know the day brings a ton
Of happiness to everyone
I'm back, full of joy and glee
Because I have the sun and the sun has me.

Rachel Bricklebank (13)
Sheffield High School, Sheffield

9/11

The day hath come, 9/11
Not a normal Tuesday
For this day will be remembered
For the years on their way.

The towers stood tall in plain view
Until the planes did come
When all that hard work was destroyed
And so their lives for some.

The day hath come, 9/11
Not a normal Tuesday
For this day will be remembered
For the years on their way.

Down the rubble fell to the ground
Destroyed all in its way
Down many fell from the big heights
Oh, what a bad, bad day!

The day hath come, 9/11
Not a normal Tuesday
For this day will be remembered
For the years on their way.

The sirens did make a big sound
As people shouted out,
'We're trying, we're trying,' they shout
But failed them in doubt.

The day hath come, 9/11
Not a normal Tuesday
For this day will be remembered
For the years on their way.

The relatives did weep and mourn
Mr Bush was so shocked
'What are we gonna do about this?'
The air flights were then stopped.

The day hath come, 9/11
Not a normal Tuesday
For this day will be remembered
For the years on their way.

Olivia Noble (13)
Sheffield High School, Sheffield

Fire

Fire always stays the same
No matter where you are
Light and burning bright
Just like the sun, our star.

The smoke curls and swirls
Black, black as night
But it is nothing compared with the flame
With such a beautiful light.

The fire crackles
Sparks bouncing high
Burning down to embers
But the flame can never die.

Something, somewhere
Is burning ever so bright
Bringing comfort or despair
With its dark, but powerful light.

Nobody can tame it
No matter how hard they try
They think they have it conquered
But fire can only be shy.

Bouncing back when you least expect
Maybe it's just play
Then returning to its coal dust cage
Not coming out again today.

Lynne Shackshaft (13)
Sheffield High School, Sheffield

The Tsunami

On the 26th December
In the year of '04
A tsunami struck south Asia
A holiday place no more.

On a sunny day it started
Where everything was well
The palm trees waved, the warm sand shone
But soon it became Hell.

This big wave started in the sea
We thought we would be safe
Unaware of this disaster
On the beach we were placed.

Across the beach we heard a cry
Coming from a small girl
Explaining about this big wave
Which was about to hurl

'Ordinary this wave is not
I learnt about in class
A tsunami this one is called
And this you may not last!'

To the mountains we fled and fled
Thousands of us were there
Enjoy was not the word to say
Neither was stop and stare

Many survived this awful day
Sadly some men did not
I was incredibly lucky
My friends won't be forgot

To a better place they have gone
A better place to dwell
I hope they shall enjoy themselves
As they are not in Hell

This 26th of December
In the year of '04
Was certainly like no other
That I had seen before.

Alice Strong (13)
Sheffield High School, Sheffield

The Lighthouse

Two miles from humanity
I live in a different world
Where light is our life
And other's lives as well.

Coming home from school
My heart beating its own pace
I can see the sea
And the sea I can taste.

I can hear the sea
Thundering against the boulders
Fathers at the machines
Sitting with hunched shoulders.

Mothers in the kitchen
Working as well
Lobster is in the frying pan
That's what I can smell.

Then I turn to the stairway
Spiralling up, up and up
Then I dive into my bedroom
Cool walls at my touch.

Yes, I live in a lighthouse
A great monster by the sea
But I am still normal
Well, as normal as can be.

Sarah Felicity Talbot (13)
Sheffield High School, Sheffield

The Tsunami

The 26th of December
In 2004
A tsunami rose from the sea
Disaster, ever more.

It struck in the Indian Ocean
Off the coast of Thailand
A forty-foot wall of water
Came bursting up the sand.

Some sunbathers ran to high land
As others stood and gazed
Shock and horror on their faces
Absolute amazed.

People hurrying everywhere
Whilst some lay on the ground
Children screaming for their parents
Not going to be found.

The ones who were not quick enough
Got swept up by the tide
Women screaming for their loved ones
Who would soon lose their lives

The town was soon swamped with water
Quickening down the streets
The only sound that could be heard
Was the stampede of their feet.

The safety crews were soon about
Searching for survivors
Scanning the flowing black waters
With local advisors.

There were thousands of survivors
Over 10,000 died
Last words to their loves ones would be,
'Till you're next by my side . . . '

Olivia Roberts (13)
Sheffield High School, Sheffield

The Oil Leak In America

Just off the coast of Louisiana
A disaster is at sea
Something is coming through the waves
Hurting nature dangerously.

The golden sand and blue sea
And clear waves that crash against the rocks
Are no more due to the terrible
Ships that leave the docks.

They travel round the world with goods
Getting large amounts of cash
But they never think about
The habitats they smash.

The oil is like an octopus
With arms that spread along the sea
Grabbing creatures' lives
It's a disaster really.

Some people were sad and shocked
Some people were quite mad
But some just sit back and say
It's really not that bad.

People tried to fix the leak
To try and stop the pollution
But the plan failed unfortunately
And led to more destruction.

Others cared for the animals
The birds and first
They had to scrub and scrub some more
To wash off the worst.

I hope this shows you just what
You are doing to your world
Think about the seas
Where the poisonous oil has swirled.

Elizabeth Rawson (13)
Sheffield High School, Sheffield

The Plane Disaster

The end of summer '86
The clouds lingered sadly
Bitterly cold was the night air
But you set off gladly.

You weren't meant to board that plane
But you and your company flew
The last flight of your life it was
As the wind howled and blew.

You set off hoping for the best
Not knowing for the worst
But then as fog and cloud thickened
A wall of grey you burst.

Dazed and disorientated
The plane lost much control
Twisting and turning to their death
They hit the ground and roll

Your girl stood waiting on the hill
She was waiting there for hours
You only left a swirl of grey
Plummeting with power.

The light was fading rapidly
She awaited her love
But as he was not returning
Dark was the sky above.

Long hours and hours passed on
She new something was wrong
And as she stared over the hill
There the damage was strong.

The end of summer '86
The clouds lingered sadly
Silence filled the bitter cold air
Returning not gladly.

Amadora Frogson (13)
Sheffield High School, Sheffield

Grandad

He walks along the street each day
Everything always fine
My grandad gives a bright, big smile
This makes him really shine.

But as the time passes right by
We hope that he'll survive
For cancer has struck in his heart
And is threatening his life.

Desperately each day we pray
For we do not know when
This disease affects many lives
And Grandad's could soon end.

Terrified he could really go
I clutch onto his arm
I don't want to ever leave him
But then there's the alarm.

As the nurses rush to his side
I'm pushed back far behind
From the glass window all I think
Are bad thoughts through my mind.

As many tears roll down my face
I start to wonder why
Who would do this to my grandad?
How can this be goodbye?

Just as we enter my grandad's room
My mum breaks down in tears
I don't feel so strong anymore
His death is now right here.

And there he lies so still for once
More tears stream down my face
My grandad has gone far away
But to a better place.

Siobhan Prentice (13)
Sheffield High School, Sheffield

A Ballad About The Twin Towers

Everyone dreaded this day
Some say it was like Hell
Others were left shocked and amazed
A huge story to tell.

The 11th of September
A normal working day
Little did anybody know
What was coming their way.

The mighty, majestic Twin Towers
Reaching up to the sky
People were ignorant inside
The towers that were high.

The disaster was impending
Two jet planes flying near
Then the catastrophe happened
Anybody could hear.

Twin Towers came crumbling down
Just within one hour
The buildings quickly demolished
Rocks as fine as flour.

Who was to blame for this tragedy?
Those on the terrorists' side
They saw it fit and for their cause
Innocent people died.

Families lost their loved ones
They are in misery
The day that scarred people for life
That went down in history.

Felicia Bi (12)
Sheffield High School, Sheffield

The Haiti Earthquake

The earth moves, the floor shakes
The buildings shudder and crumble
The wake of the earthquake
The town was covered in rubble

Belongings, thrown away
Confusion, it was all unclear
The homes taken away
The surroundings of fear

Eerie silence was there
A large cloud of dust filled the air
The emerging people
With the cries of grief and despair

Cries from under the ground
Day by day, they became weaker
Believing they were done
This city had become bleaker

They searched for helpful signs
But the ground was covered in dints
All to the innocent
All this happened in Port Au Prince

Many Haitians survived
And for those who were saved not
Those who didn't make it
These people will not be forgot

Rescuers came and left
Pulling people out of this Hell
Oh, how they tried and tried
And this was a story to tell.

Nadeen Jawad (12)
Sheffield High School, Sheffield

The Ballad Of The Prime Minister Elections

Three men, yet one Prime Minister
Which man would get the job?
Each one desperate for that place
How could they impress the nation?

One old man is named Gordon Brown
One named David Cameron
One man is named Nick Clegg
Each one capable to get the position.

Poor people eager for money
Young students looking for jobs
Children looking for education
Grandparents looking for heed.

Families' lives were destroyed from
The disastrous downturn
Which man could help these unfortunate people?
How could they lend a hand?

Now there is a battle debate
To see who'll get the job
People begging for their man
To be the Prime Minister of England.

Three men desperate not to lose
Praying to win the chair
Wanting to help the people
And make the country in good strength.

Day and night the nation voting
For the world to transform
Their lives will revolutionise
From just one vote.

Daniz Mobayen (13)
Sheffield High School, Sheffield

A Ballad Of The Titanic

On a dark night, April 1912
A disaster out at sea
A ship, the Titanic, it was called
But clearly they couldn't see

Large white icebergs up ahead of them
So their radars failed to seek
The crash was very close to midnight
The temperatures were so bleak.

A few hours later that morning
When they saw they were sinking
Some people started to scream and shout
The captain without blinking

He tried hard to steer the ship away
But saw that it was no use
The steering of the ship was failing
To move it just refused

The big ship was sinking deeper down
People jumped overboard
The sea was flowing in
The Titanic couldn't be restored

Then the lifeboats were launched from the ship
People were swimming away
The big ship was sinking so far down
Right down towards the seabed.

So many people went down that day
Few managed to survive
Because in the lifeboats they escaped
Though so many did die.

Rebecca Higgins (12)
Sheffield High School, Sheffield

Disaster In New York

In 2000 the planes did strike
The Twin Towers of New York
Watching as the clouds filled with ash
As the terrorists brought

The terror started after that
As 5,000 were struck
Gazing down at the followers
The 3,000 were took.

Their short lives lived uncompleted
Survivors trapped inside
Thinking of ways to flee the fire
Putting all fears aside.

Helpers, families of ones trapped
Stood helplessly and wept
Most praying, putting faith in God
As secrets remained kept.

The bravest of New York city
Risked their lives to save all
For no more tragedy
Hoping to end this war.

Burning rubble left in the air
People left just to stare
Helpless, jumping down from the blocks
Laying with a deathly glare.

As families left in despair
Nightmares to remember
Children left without parents
Hearts were broken that September.

Sophia Livoti (13)
Sheffield High School, Sheffield

Sheffield Floods

It happened in the month of June
That terrible disaster
The rain did not stop pouring
It got faster and faster.

It began very early morning
And did not stop for a week
People's homes and lives were destroyed
It left their homes dark and bleak.

The people they were greatly shocked
As no warning was given
The floods they were unwanted there
Some parts became forbidden.

Their homes were completely destroyed
For many it would be a long time
Before they could live there again
They had to draw a line.

Many things were lost that day
For a few it was their lives
But for lots it was treasured things
For men it was their wives.

That terrible month of June
The worst month of some's lives
All we can do is hope and pray
For those who lost their lives.

Grace Shurmer (13)
Sheffield High School, Sheffield

My Ballad Of An Earthquake

The innocent people were unaware
No one will have seen it coming
So in the month of January
A disaster was approaching.

The ground had become an African snake
The people started to awake
Their lives had become a living nightmare
The small island began to quake.

Their houses and belongings were destroyed
Some lay there under the rubble
Some injured and needing help and safety
They didn't ask for much trouble.

They were left homeless and orphans
Their lives were ruined already
They had emergency kits sent to them
And the help needed was steady.

Around the world people gave sympathy
They truly felt for the homeless
So they fundraised and collected money
And they gave Haiti their blessing.

We all made donations to the Haitians
And their lives are being restored
And hopefully they will recover it
That's a historical record.

Humera Riaz (13)
Sheffield High School, Sheffield

Hurricanes?

One afternoon watching the telly
Hearing news of a hurricane
What should I do in this terrible trauma?
A hurricane is waiting to pounce.

Hearing news of a hurricane
Screams and shouts I hear
A hurricane is waiting to pounce
What have I done so wrong in my life?

Screams and shouts I hear
Sadness has filled the air
What have I done so wrong in my life?
How could no one care?

Sadness has filled the air
Laughter seems long gone
How could no one care?
Great people are about to die.

Laughter seems long gone
Sadness has replaced it
Great people are about to die
And lose their world forever.

Sadness has replaced happiness
Hearing news of a hurricane
Losing people's world forever
Watching the telly one afternoon.

Abbie Danielle Linell (13)
Sheffield High School, Sheffield

Sad Surprise

My long day was bad already
On my way home from camp
My friend threw up all over me
Ending up green and damp.

When I thought it would get better
My thoughts were deeply wrong
A small shoebox waited for me
Tiny and not too long.

I opened it to see inside
My guinea big, poor thing
I stroked its velvet, floppy ears
The coldness like a sting.

A single tear rolled down my cheek
I'd just lost my best friend
He had always been there for me
Never thought it would end.

I closed the lid, picked up the box
Carried it to the door
I dug a hole and put it in
I cried and cried some more.

I said a few words to myself
About the times we shared
How he was always there for me
The one who only cared.

Tegan Caddy (13)
Sheffield High School, Sheffield

Things Aren't What They Seem

In a town, village, city or place
Where people run and people race
There's more to a friend than meets the eye
So come into my dream and I.

Where seagulls run and humans fly
And children hush and adults cry
So come into my dream and I
There's more to the world than meets the eye.

No need to run, no need to hide
Just pick up a board and learn to glide
In a town, village, city or place
Don't rush the time, just take your pace

Where lions are predators and humans are prey
And statues are real and toys are clay
So come into my dream and I
There's more to the Earth than meets the eye.

Fire enraged with heavy flames
And water too large to claim
In a town, village, city or place
You don't have to run to set a pace.

Where fish can run for eternity
And birds can swim with great energy
In a town, village, city or place
You don't have to be fast to win the race.

Olivia Beavers (13)
Sheffield High School, Sheffield

Baby P Ballad

Little P, did anyone know?
He lay there broken-limbed
The case did cause shock and concern
The tale spread around like wind.

Fractured ribs and a ruptured heart
Many hospital trips
The seventeen month-old baby
Never got his cheek kissed.

Why did this poor baby get harmed?
How could someone do this?
He didn't do anything wrong
He had no life of bliss.

The story was judged by the court
The mother plead with guilt
Child carers were widely concerned
Many tears were spilt.

The news was published everywhere
Piles of papers were bought
The whole wide world inside and out
A sad, lonely life cut short.

He died on the 3rd of August
A teddy bear in hand
Please let Baby P rest in peace
Regret throughout the land.

Charlotte Farrugia (13)
Sheffield High School, Sheffield

Jack The Ripper Ballad

In the year 1888
A dead body was found
A woman aged twenty-seven
Was spotted on the ground

She was not the first to be killed
There were many more deaths
Six young women to be precise
All breathed their final breaths.

The assassin, Jack the Ripper
No one knew who he was
The police had no idea
Who was breaking their laws.

Although there was no evidence
Who was the real killer
People still talked about who did it
In this real life thriller.

The police got many letters
Most were thought to be fake
A great number were thrown away
But was that a mistake?

People very often forget
All the women who died
They were members of families too
Mothers, daughters and wives.

Wankumbu Chisala (13)
Sheffield High School, Sheffield

The 9/11 Twin Towers

September 2001
Destruction descended
As chaos, havoc and carnage
Occurred and lives ended.

The Twin Towers were invaded
By two planes which collide
On the orders of terrorists
Who then escaped to hide.

Thousands of deaths were created
Passengers on the planes
Office workers in the buildings
Their fate was all the same.

The scope of devastation
Overwhelmed the whole world
As most of New York was destroyed
And horror unfurled.

The American responded
By declaring a war
On Al-Qaeda terrorists
As this was the last straw.

The 11th September
When trust was dismembered
Thousands of lives were affected
Always to be remembered.

Kazna Asker (13)
Sheffield High School, Sheffield

The Great Fire Of London Ballad

Well, it started in September
In 1666
When the maid left on the ovens
After she made breadsticks.

Then the heat started to ignite
Grey smoke soon spread to flames
The kitchen was quickly perished
The maid was in deep shame.

The kitchen collapsed in ashes
The bakery was alight
The people of London were shocked
They cried and hurried that night.

All things good and bad were charred
The city was quite bare
Like looking at a sheet of black
Ash and dust everywhere.

Nobody knew how it started
Except the maid herself
Now London was blazing, red-hot
She lost everyone's wealth.

Family and friends suffered great loss
And many pigeons died
All because of a silly mistake
Only a few survived.

Molly Norman & Melissa White (13)
Sheffield High School, Sheffield

Places I Know

I know a place where the ospreys fly
And the squirrels twitch
And the reindeer sigh
This is a place I know.

I know a place where the dolphins leap
And the lobsters crawl
And the willows weep
This is a place I know.

I know a place where the people buzz
And the whales beach
And the sky's a fuzz
This is a place I know.

I know a place where the water is black
And the ground is barren
And one can't go back
This is depression, I know.

But I know a place where the air is pure
And there is no doubt
And there are no wars
There exists no sadness
Just jubilation and gladness
To this place, one day, I'll go.

Juliet Armstrong (13)
Sheffield High School, Sheffield

The Hedgehog

Crouched on a lonely lane
The jewelled stars blinking above him
He observes the wind-blown grass.

The moon shimmers like a silver sea
A blinding light slices through the road
His spiky armour won't save him now.

Trishna Kurian (12)
Sheffield High School, Sheffield

High Above

I'm high above
Soaring, I can see for miles around
This is a strange experience for me
Since I am human

Soaring, I can see for miles around
From high above I see ant-like creatures
Since I am human
Flying doesn't seem right

From high above I see ant-like creatures
It feels like I have the world in my hand
Flying doesn't seem right
But I don't want to stop.

It feels like I have the world in my hand
I can fly to the moon and touch the stars
But I don't want to stop
I don't want to touch the ground.

I'm walking on air
This is a strange experience for me
But even though I'm human
I'm high above.

Nikita Azeem (13)
Sheffield High School, Sheffield

The Bee

Sucking, secret, silent
Unaware of all but sweetness
Oblivious, even to its bright background
He shuffles back, like a baby crawls and flies.

He is the messenger, he leaves his gift
Then off he goes, over slated, slanting floors
To his mother, the mother of thousands.

Frances Anderson (12)
Sheffield High School, Sheffield

Welcome To A Special Place

Welcome to a special place
Where horses talk
And snails walk
Welcome to a special place.

Welcome to a crazy world
Where cats chase dogs
And sun is fog
Welcome to a crazy world.

Welcome to a mixed-up town
Where kings are poor
And spiders roar
Welcome to a mixed-up town.

Welcome to a different planet
Where money's worthless
And pizza's priceless
Welcome to a different planet.

Welcome to Crunchieland
Where black is white
And left is right
Welcome to Crunchieland!

Holly West (12)
Sheffield High School, Sheffield

The Cat

He listens quietly with pricked-up ears
Close to midnight his prey appears
Surrounded by darkness, he hears.

His sharp eyes locked on where he lay
There in the pretty garden was his prey
He pounces, bounds and leaps away.

Olivia Pryor (13)
Sheffield High School, Sheffield

Greenflies

I am sat on the grass with my friends and my family
Some of my friends, include Sophie and Emily
The greenfly is flying in the cool, open air
But it's buzzed far away now and it's over there

It is happily flying into my open mouth
Stupid greenflies make us sad
And sometimes we will shout
The greenfly is flying from far up to here
Please go away, because you're getting too near

Now we caught it and trapped it
Ha, ha, ha, Mr Fly
But Sophie protested
And little Emily cried
The greenfly is gone now so there's no need to fret
Sophie said, 'But you guys, he was somebody's pet.'

Now we all feel terrible, we can't murder a fly
Sophie did have a point, he did not need to die
So we set him free and he flew far away
And tomorrow I'll cry for remember today.

Sarah Lee-Liggett (12)
Sheffield High School, Sheffield

The Arabian Stallion

I may see him trotting on a sandy shore
I may see him trotting on an uphill moor.

I may see him neighing on a Sheffield street
I may see him neighing with a flock of sheep.

But I do not see him at the Bakewell Show
There are other breeds, both high and low.

My favourite bred of horse
Has to be, of course
The Arabian stallion.

Emma Nicole Spencer (13)
Sheffield High School, Sheffield

Waiting To Die

I lie here, waiting to die
I want to laugh and I want to cry
I want to dance and I want to groove
But what can I do, when I can't even move?

Death may be early, it may be late
But all I can do is lie here and wait
I want to rejoice the last moments of my life
The joy I have been through, the anger and strife.

Every second, is agonising me
I need to unlock my troubles with a happiness key
I want to start afresh, making no mistakes
Let my sadness fall asleep and my gladness awake.

I'm not scared of death anymore
Because I know I'll open another door
I can feel the darkness engulfing me
But I see a light and I know I am free!

Tanvi Acharya (13)
Sheffield High School, Sheffield

Trying To Write A Poem

I'm trying to write a poem for school
But I really don't know what to say
Everything I write sounds like the words of a fool
Maybe I'll find the right words some day.

I could write about the weather
I could write about an animal
I could write about a feather
Or I could write about a mammal.

Although an idea springs to mind
The more I sit and puzzle
I shall write about how hard I find
Writing poems without a struggle!

Sophie Peckett (12)
Sheffield High School, Sheffield

It Is Silent

Leaves on the trees drift silently down
Around me there is not a sound
A beautiful bird swoops gracefully down
It is silent.

Around me there is not a sound
Light dapples the rocky ground
It is silent
In my mystical world.

Light dapples the rocky ground
Water trickles by without a sound
In my mystical world
The animals run freely.

Water trickles by without a sound
Leaves on the trees drift silently down
The animals run freely
A beautiful bird swoops gracefully down.

Roshni Timms (13)
Sheffield High School, Sheffield

Who Am I?

You are often scared of me
But I can help you actually.
As you sit and wait
You hope that things are running late.
I like to keep all things clean
And I promise you I'm not that mean.
I always wear a big white mask
And with the job comes a task.
What else could I be
But a dentist? Can't you see.

Georgia Tracey & Sarah Throssell (11)
Sheffield High School, Sheffield

The Trees, They Tell Me Secrets

I can feel the glistening raindrops
Cold and damp on my fingertips
The wind is whistling softly
And the trees, they tell me secrets.

Cold and damp on my fingertips
When the moon shivers at night
Pieces of silver tingle my nose
More like pieces of a miniature Heaven.

More like pieces of a miniature Heaven
Clouds call birds to the air
The water is like a million horses
Galloping with mighty courage.

Now the night is at rest
And the wind is whistling softly
The animals prowl or howl
As the trees, they tell me secrets.

Lara Conboy (13)
Sheffield High School, Sheffield

The Lighthouse

My house isn't like your house
My house is red and white
My house protects boats from their destination
My house shines like a star in the night sky
My house is a lighthouse.

Sarah Anne Myers (13)
Sheffield High School, Sheffield

The Chicken

She pecks and picks corn off the ground
All the hens scurry around
She is an apple bobber

She lives in a market place
Where she is always short of space
Oh how she wishes she was free range.

She could run and she would be so free
Just with her friends, how happy she'd be
But no, she is trapped.

An egg she carries deep inside
She hides it so it is not fried
Just until it's hatched.

And when it is, she thinks quietly
They will probably just eat me
Good luck my little baby.

Jessica Askham (12)
Sheffield High School, Sheffield

Winter Poem

To go to bed at night, to a world in desperate plight
Financial ruin, bombers in flight, Brown's on the telly
The nation in blight, and wake in the morning
God's put it to right
Snow on the fields, robins in sight
Bare trees, barren of leaves
Spring back to beauty, covered in snow
A joy to behold, a wondrous sight
Nine inches of snow and try as we might
Our road is blocked
No school, oh delight.

Tobogganing, snowmen, igloos, snow fights
The children think the snow's a delight
The grown-ups however, a much different view
No work or pay, abandon the car
And that is all I have so far.

Eleanor Hyde (11)
Sheffield High School, Sheffield

Politics

Labour is a red rose
That gets up people's nose
The Tories are a tree
They sting like a bee
Lib-Dems are a bird
They like following the herd
BNP are the Union Jack
They want immigrants to go back
UKIP are the pound
They are hounds
Green is the flower
They're never gonna be in power
But all this politics stuff
Really gets me in a huff!

Jonty Farmer (12)
Sir Graham Balfour School, Stafford

The Sea And Me

I calmly floated out to sea,
Just my little boat and me,
The waves are smooth and all so kind,
I wonder through my empty mind.

I hear no words, I see no fear,
My mind is empty and so clear,
I hope for a future and happy one too,
One that involves only me and you.

My little boat is green and bright,
Shining out through all the night.
Still I float through all the sea,
It's just my little boat and me.

The waves hit hard, I'm sinking fast,
I thought about the clearing past,
My mum is there, my sister too,
There's someone else, I don't know who.

My boat has crashed I fall out,
I sit and listen to the echoed shout,
A shout for help and I'm on my feet,
I'm running in the burning heat.

I look around, this little isle,
Some sticks and stones are in a pile,
I'm in a shelter, someone's there,
Someone who does really care.

Now I live upon this beautiful isle,
I'll walk around with a big smile,
The birds will sing and dance along,
They'll join me in this little song.

I'm happy here and for all I care,
This little isle I will always share.

Charlotte Hall (13)
Sir Graham Balfour School, Stafford

My Best Friend!

Fluffy and soft, smooth and light,
He cuddles me tight in the night,
Caring for me, in his own little way,
Begging for food and for me to stay.

When we go shopping we go on the bus,
We sit at the back and I give him a fuss.
I love my dog, he's mine forever,
I'll leave him never ever.

Let me tell you that he is mine,
No need for vets, as he is fine,
His name is very special to me,
As his name is Barny!

Listen to his loud, soft bark,
A spot on his back is a birth mark.
Run around and throw a frisbee,
A rough, long tongue softly licks me.

As a puppy, he looked so cute,
He listens to me when I play the flute.
His wet paws all over the floor,
And jumping up at the back door.

He runs to me when I get home,
So I gently brush him with a comb,
We lie on the sofa and watch TV,
I change the channel and turn on 'Glee'.

I put Barny in his bed,
And gently stroke his little head.
I kiss him and say goodnight,
As I turn off the kitchen light.

My best friend, I love him so dear,
Every second I want to keep him near!

Kiera Robinson (13)
Sir Graham Balfour School, Stafford

Liberty Is Mine
(I was inspired to write this after listening to 'The Best Day' - a song by my favourite singer, Taylor Swift)

All my life has been an adventure,
All my life I've drawn close to one person
He is my day, my night,
My dark, my light.
He makes me feel like a bird in the sky
I'm free, liberty is mine.

I'm 5 years old . . .

We're in the orchard, I hear him laugh,
I smile at him.
He starts to chase me.
I run through the autumn wind
I am free, liberty is mine.

I'm 13 years old . . .

My friends hate me, I can't breathe.
I come home crying and you hug me as if I were a cuddly bear
We get in the car and drive away
To a town far, far away
We talk and talk until I forget all about my day,
He makes me feel free, liberty is mine.

I'm 15 now . . .

I may have guessed this mystic truth
Of how my father is my youth
He makes me feel so warm inside
And I have left my past behind.
I made new friends and lived my life
To the full as if I were free, as if liberty was mine.

Erin Softley (13)
Sir Graham Balfour School, Stafford

Animals - Keep Them Alive

There are many animals
In this world
They are all amazing
Just like you and me
I would name them all
But that would take too long to write
So I'm just gonna tell you
Why they should stay alive
It is not right to kill
We should all know that
But we still kill
Just to have a nice dinner
I do not like it
That is why I'm a veggie
Please don't kill
It would make me happy
Just think what the animal is thinking
They do not want to die
Think what would happen if they all went
This planet would then have a big dent
We would then have nothing to look at in awe
All our lives would be such a bore
I know we kill to survive
And they do too
But we have shops with different food in
And they do not
There are many animals
In this world
Please keep them alive.

Katie Nichol (13)
Sir Graham Balfour School, Stafford

Farm Frenzy

Down on the farm we farm
All the bales are in the barn
All the cows in the shed
The lazy farmers are in bed
Early in the morning we get up
To circumcise the tup
The tractors we own growl
The smell from the cow shed is foul
We shear the sheep
Few lambs we actually keep
The rest go to market
The truck, I need to learn to park it

When it comes to planting spuds
This is when all the ground usually floods
Throughout the year the sprayer comes out
It breaks down, give it a clout
Then when it comes to harvest time
Revving our engines is no crime
We dig the spuds and cut the corn
Once we're finished a new farming year is born
In winter we grin and bear it
We hope to get our hands on some grit
The frost comes hard
All over the yard
The cows get brought in out of the cold
'Don't give up,' we get told.
Well there you have it, the farmers' year
Flippin 'eck I need a beer!

Rob Bowyer (13)
Sir Graham Balfour School, Stafford

View Of The Battle

The death rattle of the machine gun,
The thrill of the rush.
The sprint ahead,
The cold wet touch.
The thought of dread,
Of those who are dead,
And those there are too much.

The voices call out,
The loud shout,
The screams of pain and misery,
The fallen men,
Count ten, and ten,
This becomes a familiar fight.

The bullets fly
The echo keeps ringing,
The suffocating tie,
The coughing preaching.
The bodies that are bloodshot,
And the heads that are destroyed,
They wait for the colonel's nod.

For me life is now a game,
A fight for freedom once again.
The scars that scare me forever,
Will leave me never ever.
The war is a dark disease,
I wish it to leave me,
Please, oh please.

Charlotte Forrester (13)
Sir Graham Balfour School, Stafford

Room 302

I kick at the chains,
I look through the peephole,
They give me migraines,
All of these dead people.
There's red writing all over my door,
Is it blood or ink?
I keep hearing roars,
And there is a bad stink,
My walls scream,
The clock endlessly tocks,
I have such bad dreams,
I'm trapped by the locks.
I wish I was deaf and blind,
Then I could be alone,
Have peace of mind,
And not breaking bones,
If I went into the bathroom,
Into the strange hole,
I'd meet my doom,
I'd lose my soul.
Many, many screaming babies,
Oh no,
A zombie dog with rabies!
Thank God they're slow.
I watch murders of innocent people,
I'm 21121,
The fall of a church steeple,
And a barrel of a gun.

Tamsin Tolfree (12)
Sir Graham Balfour School, Stafford

The Sea

The sea can be like many things:

Sometimes, it's like an eagle,
Striking swiftly, grasping its prey and baring it down,
Its darting eyes seeing all intruders,
Sometimes forgiving, but often not.

Then, it can be like a wolf,
Hunting by night on easy prey,
Crushing victims in strong jaws,
Then resting afterwards, suddenly calm,
And like the wolf, it's top of the food chain.

Next, it could be like a leopard,
Jumping up high to grab its prey off rocks,
Untameable and uncontrollable,
Following the orders of no one,
Knowing no right or wrong.

Suddenly, it resembles closely to a horse,
Beautiful but dangerous,
Forgiving to those intruders,
But not to those who seek to harm,
Instead trampling them with crashing waves.

The sea can be like many things,
Which change with its many different moods,
It's totally unpredictable,
And never has or will be changed.

Oliver McCoy (13)
Sir Graham Balfour School, Stafford

The Nature Of Our World

I love the way the trees blow in the wind,
The way the leaves gently flutter down.
I love the way the sun sets red,
It's a time when your face can't bear a frown.
I love the way the lakes are sparkly blue,
And in the spring, there are baby ewes.
I love the way the grass smells fresh,
And the way the birds come out just for you.

I love the way the snow feels on my skin,
The way it's as delicate as glass.
I love the way the frost clings to your body,
And the way the dew sets on the grass.
I love the way snow is like a blanket on the ground,
And the way that you can see your footprints on the floor.
I love the way robins fly in the sky,
The way you can't wait for what winter has in store!

I love the way the sun beats down on you in the summer,
And the way the ice cream dribbles down your hand.
I love the way the sea smells fresh,
Your skin, under the sun, is tanned.
I love the way the cold breezes cool you down,
And the way the wind is twirled.
I love the feel of nature at my fingertips,
And how this is our world.

Sarina Patel (13)
Sir Graham Balfour School, Stafford

Acting Against Child Abuse

Tied up by a rusty chain,
A lonely child screams in pain.
Scars that ruin her pretty face,
The same old dress,
Blood-covered lace.

She should've told us,
I know she should,
But if she'd have tried I doubt she could.

And now she's here,
Battered and bruised,
There's not much left now for her to lose.

Hit by a rope,
Harder and harder,
The evil face of her angry father.
Tears are pouring from her eyes,
No one to answer her desperate cries.

Too much pain, too much abuse,
If she's offered help she has to refuse.
She can't describe the voices she's hearing.

It's too late now,
She's disappearing.

Stephanie Essery (13)
Sir Graham Balfour School, Stafford

The Ballerina

As she turns and twirls across the floor,
She jumps and leaps and twirls some more.
Her small tutu flaps up and down,
As she skips around without a frown.
She pas-de-chats and pirouettes,
She points her toes, without a sweat.
Her feet are sore, her arms aching,
But she looks well, her skill of faking.
On her pointes she spins around,
With only two toes on the ground.
Her body weight rests on her toes,
How much it hurts nobody knows.
And from classical to contemporary,
She flies around like a canary.
She triple runs across the room,
She sweeps around just like a broom.
Her arms change shape with lots of grace,
A big, friendly smile upon her face.
She ends her routine with a leap in the air,
The amount of talent she has is unfair.
And out of the tutu, out of mode ballerina,
She is just a normal teenage girl called Marina.

Kayleigh Steel (13)
Sir Graham Balfour School, Stafford

Friends

Sometimes you just need friends,
You need them to comfort you,
You need them to make you laugh,
You need them to make you smile when you're down.

My friends mean the world to me,
The way that they are always there for me,
No matter what,
My friends are like my family.

I admire the way your friends stick up for you, if you're having a rough time.
I find it great how they always compliment you, even if you don't exactly look like a million dollars!

However,
I hate it when we fall out,
I hate it when we fight,
I hate it when we don't talk to each other,
I don't like falling out with my friends; it makes me feel sad, and unhappy.
Like I am not one of them anymore.

My friends mean the world to me, I love my friends.

Ella Platt
Sir Graham Balfour School, Stafford

A Dog Death

My dog died last November
My best friend for sixteen years
We were born the same month
It was April
Now I cannot stop crying

It is not fair
That dogs die young
Just a tiny part of our lives
They give us happiness and joy
To the elderly and young particularly

More loyal than human affection
More passionate and caring
Any upsetting time
Was removed by my dog

My grief is extreme
My terror is strong
None will be removed
Without this creature.

His name was
Larry the Labrador.

Toby Hollinshead (13)
Sir Graham Balfour School, Stafford

Music

Music is like your own language,
Its lyrics like a story you have lived your life within
Sometimes it seems that song was written for you,
Because everything it talks about, you have been through.

Music gives me an adrenaline rush,
The beat bouncing everything around.
I sing for my life, like nothing can stop me,
I dance for my life, like nothing will stop me!

The melody carries on in my head,
Keeping me going through the day,
It picks me up and spins me round,
I can't help but tap my foot to its sound.

My life is built around music,
I get home from a busy day,
And have a boogie to a bit of R 'n' B
The house echoing it around me.

We are the generation of music!

Poppy Fletcher (13)
Sir Graham Balfour School, Stafford

Infinite

As it drifts across a black obis,
Slowly, silently, secretly, it turns and topples, getting smaller every second.

They have taken many lives and many ships,
But none last forever, you will never see two,
All icebergs will end their lives on that one final turn,
Dissolving, descending, degrading.

Oliver Dracup-Nicholls (13)
Sir Graham Balfour School, Stafford

Dreams

To visit many countries
To ride the London Eye
To eat in an American diner
And to see an eagle fly

To go on a holiday to the Seychelles
To be able to speak fluent Maltese
To swim with dolphins in Florida
And to try and swing on a trapeze

To bungee jump from a bridge
To adopt a rescue animal
To go down a zip wire
And to go and see the Taj Mahal

To climb a mountain abroad
To be part of some teams
To visit the Empire State Building
And to fulfil all of these dreams.

Valentina Calleja (13)
Sir Graham Balfour School, Stafford

Once I'm In My Bubble Bath

Once I'm in my bubble bath,
I like to stir up more,
Half the bubbles go in my eyes,
And half go on the floor.

The fun is in the bubbles,
The giggle on my skin,
And when I stick them to my face,
They dangle off my chin.

And when I splash them hard enough,
They pop and disappear,
And then my bathtime's over 'cause,
I have made the bath go clear.

Emma Forrester (13)
Sir Graham Balfour School, Stafford

Sisters

Sisters are special, right from the start,
They're always there to hold your hand, and reach into your heart.
My sister is one of a kind, she simply is the best,
And if you dare to hurt her, it is you that I'll detest.

My sister isn't perfect, she can sometimes be wrong,
We can fall out and have arguments, but they never last that long.
I've learnt a lot from others, by looking up to them,
But no one can compare to you, because you're my special gem.

As sisters we've been through a lot, we've made it through thick and thin,
But think of all our memories, I wouldn't know where to begin.
Sisters are for life, what more could I ask for?
Together forever and hand in hand, do we really need any more?

Now that we're together, and even if we're apart,
We will always be close at mind and even closer in our hearts.

Jemma Barlow (13)
Sir Graham Balfour School, Stafford

Cry A Little, Laugh A Lot

Cry a little, laugh a lot
Is what I like to say
'Cause no one should be sad
They should be happy every day

Cry a little, laugh a lot
Is what I have told you now
I think you should only cry
If you have said, 'Owww!'

Cry a little, laugh a lot
Is what I have said
Think about what I have told you
And keep it in your head.

Flo Peczek (13)
Sir Graham Balfour School, Stafford

Good Times

First there's winter
Coldest time of the year,
Then there's spring
Easter eggs here we come,
Next is summer
Kicking the cold,
Last is autumn
Watch those leaves fall.

First there's Easter
Eating chocolate,
Then there's holiday
Time for rest,
Next there's Halloween
Try to give a scare,
Last there's Christmas
Singing carols.

First there's mine
Birthday time,
Then there's Ben's
Give him some hens,
Next there's Josh's
That's the posh one,
Then it's time to start all other again!

Ashley Powley (12)
Sir Henry Cooper School, Hull

The Football Game

The boys run out,
Onto the pitch,
My nerves give me,
An ominous twitch.

The game has started,
We're on a roll.
But the other team,
Has scored a goal . . .

It's half time,
Let's have a drink.
We are losing,
I'm going to shrink.

He shoots,
He scores.
'Yeah!'
The stadium roars.

It is the end,
Of the game.
I can't wait,
To come again.

Cydnee Jones (11)
Sir Henry Cooper School, Hull

That Fly . . .

As he flies,
With his beady eyes,
He sticks to me,
Like a flea,

My friend says to me,
Who is he?
He's that fly,
Who lives nearby . . .

Molly Toker (11)
Sir Henry Cooper School, Hull

There Could Be . . .

There should be a desk,
That can answer your test.

There could be a folder,
The shape of a boulder.

There shouldn't be a sock,
As hard as a rock.

There might be a town,
As silly as a clown.

There could be a tree,
The size of a bee.

There might be a mouse,
The shape of a house.

There could be a chair,
As big as a bear.

There shouldn't be a dish,
The size of a fish.

And a chocolate bar for free,
All for me!

Ellie Wetherell (12)
Sir Henry Cooper School, Hull

Rugby

Bradford, Hull, Castleford too,
Rugby enjoyment for me and you,
Leeds, Featherstone, Wigan too,
Gotta love Rugby, it's all true.
York, Saints, Toulouse too,
Good, bad teams, old and new,
Laugh, cheer, ball out too,
Rugby enjoyment for me and you!

Kane Sutherby (12)
Sir Henry Cooper School, Hull

Spring

Trees, trees in spring are bright,
Some are small, some have height.
All the pollen makes us sneeze,
Most of us are dodging bees.

Trees, trees in spring are bright,
Some are small, some have height.
Eating ice cream all day long,
Some of us like to sing songs.

Trees, trees in spring are bright,
Some are small, some have height.
Singing song birds up in trees,
Protecting their eggs from the breeze.

Trees, trees in spring are bright,
Some are small, some have height.
People walking their cute dogs,
Near the pond there are green frogs!

This is spring!

Declan Pidd (12)
Sir Henry Cooper School, Hull

The Spy

Oh no! It's the spy!
He's as cheeky as a fly,
But he's nothing like a guy.
All bold and strong,
From eating pies.
He gets his hopes up,
Very lucky and with pride!
Nearly got his victim,
Unfortunately he missed him!

So sad, so worried,
What's he going to do?
He needs you!
Poor spy - he doesn't like telling lies,
So he thinks he's gonna die!

Layla Alison (11)
Sir Henry Cooper School, Hull

Chocolate

Creamy
White
Orange and
Brown

Chocolate never
Puts me down

Caramel
Toffee
Bountys and
Cream

Every night
I dream! I dream!

Danielle Johnson (12)
Sir Henry Cooper School, Hull

World Cup Poem

In June it is the World Cup,
And England are going up!
But watch out for Spain,
They are such a pain.

In June it is the World Cup,
And Ballack will be tripped up.
Germany will be going down,
And the manager will have a frown.

In June it is the World Cup,
And England are going up.
But stay clear of France
They will have you dazzled in a trance.

James Hall (12)
Sir Henry Cooper School, Hull

When Love Is Complicated

When love is a complication
There is all you need and adore
But even though you hurt me so
I come running back for more

When love is an affliction
There is not much one can do
Despite the way you treated me
I'm still in love with you

Again, again I feel that hurt
For you I can't forsake
In which I feel in love again
And I come back for more to take

What makes me hurt so much?
That gives me this much pain and grief
You, all you,
And I must love in vain.

Jacob Seickell (14)
Solihull School, Solihull

My Sister's Room

It was the pink stethoscope,
The lone glass on the nightstand,
The silver earrings in the purse,
The photos, old and new together,
The named candles by the window.

It was the perfume and hairspray which filled the air,
The jewellery box on the corner chair,
The make-up in the bathroom,
The broken teddy in the wardrobe,
The heels by the door.

It was the mirror on the window ledge,
The mirror by the bedroom door,
The necklace on the bookcase,
The 'Twilight' books in pride of place,
The girly magazine on the bed.

It was the ballgown on the wardrobe door,
The car keys by the sink.
The iPod charging on the floor,
The mobile by the pillow,
The textbook on the rug.

It was the pink stethoscope,
The lone glass on the nightstand,
The silver earrings in the purse,
The photos, old and new together,
The named candles by the window.

Luke Carr (14)
Solihull School, Solihull

When I Was A Mill Girl

'Get out of the way!'
The demon would cry,
Whip in his hand,
Boy at his side.

His shirt is removed,
And whip lifted up,
It took one strike,
For the boy to be cut.

Then a girl screams,
The usual I guess,
Pulled in the machine,
By the thread of her dress.

It was like that for me,
When I worked at the mill,
I often collapsed,
And sometimes was ill.

Listen to my story,
My pretty little tale,
Of when I was a mill girl,
All skinny and pale.

I'd been at it for years,
And never been praised,
They say, 'Be polite,
It's the way you were raised.'

I started at five,
Finished at eight,
Beaten till black,
If you're five minutes late,

The machines were noisy,
They groaned and moaned,
They make you scared,
And want to go home.

It was hot and damp,
To stop threads from snapping,
There's the sound of the whip,
And of bones cracking.

I was there on that day,
When the girl got pulled in,
All I could see was
Shredded clothes and skin.

'They're all replaceable,'
The boss would state,
I overheard him,
From behind a gate.

I need to escape,
I often thought,
Many had tried,
But they always got caught.

I had to try,
It was so bad,
I wanted my mum,
I wanted my dad.

When no one was looking,
I fled to the door,
But it was locked
I should have guessed it before.

The window was open,
'Finally!' I cried,
I leapt out the window,
And ran to hide.

I can't believe it!
How can it be!
Phew! I thought,
And now I'm free!

Grace Lodge (13)
Solihull School, Solihull

The Grown-Up

The grown-up inside me is boring,
Or at least, it seems that way.
She likes tea with no sugar, no biscuits, no milk,
And a sit-down meal at the end of the day.

She likes vouchers and vegetable soup,
Has a neat and tidy house,
She files away her vegetables,
And squeals at every mouse.

Her best friend is her milkman,
Though she's thinking of getting a cat . . .
She'd name it Rosco or Ragmar,
And there's nothing wrong with that!

She hates the ice cream van man,
His tune should be a crime!
She often has dreams of running him down
Or choking him on a Flake '99.

She also has dreams of a maid,
And having a huge manor house
Of quitting her job in the charity shop
And buying a trendier blouse.

She dreams of finding a man
(One who doesn't smell)
Who drives a blue Mercedes
And talks of wedding bells.

She dreams of a big white wedding,
With a fleet of bridesmaids in blue
And drifting down the aisle
To the shock of the people she knew.

A honeymoon in Majorca
A baby girl or two
And a cottage down in Devon
With no city hullabaloo.

A long and happy retirement
And to die in a soft white bed
With her husband holding her hand
And no feeling of worry or dread.

But she's simply far too busy:
Her sister's visiting soon,
She's got to wash the 'fancy towels',
Because her sister's a grown-up too.

So the grown-up deep inside me
Will have to learn to stay
Because I don't want to be sorting wallpaper
When I reach her age one day.

Amy Hughes (15)
Solihull School, Solihull

The Cat

Night sneaker
Rubbish eater
Fish taker
Ornament breaker

Smile maker
Baby waker
Comfort giver
Rat deliverer

Bed warmer
Pantry stormer
Attention seeker
Sock stealer
Friendship dealer

Food muncher
Mouse puncher
Child cuddler
Cold huddler.

Oscar Street (15)
Solihull School, Solihull

Dancing Through The Rain

The hardest day of my life, yesterday came and died,
But you were there, and without you I couldn't have even tried.

You are the first one that helped me, the first to see me cry,
You're the one I can relate to,
From whom I never need hide.

Like the sister that I have never owned, you take her place,
Having the best advice and reassurance,
You're an asset to the human race.

If I ever need some cheering up, I know just who to call,
You've always been there - right from the start,
You'd never let me fall.

Being the one I can rely on, who considers everything,
You're the one that even at four in the morning,
I need not hesitate to ring.

Reminding me what I have right now, and not what I may lose,
By my side each day every hour,
You're the one I'll always choose.

You don't know how grateful I am,
For you taking away the pain,
Thank you so much for teaching me,
How to dance through the rain.

Charlotte Beesley (14)
Solihull School, Solihull

Heartbreak

I trusted you,
I thought you did me,
Everything was just perfect,
Until you said what you said.

I believed your lies,
And adored your smiles,
I thought I needed you,
Until you said what you said.

I wanted you to love me,
Although now I know you don't,
I thought I'd always love you,
Until you said what you said.

I thought you were my king,
And that I was your queen,
And that we would be together forever.
But yes, that was before you said what you said.

Lottie Wilson (14)
Solihull School, Solihull

Daffodils

Sunshine-yellow petals hanging from the silver-green shoots,
Casting shadows upon the dew-kissed blades below,
They stand proud, beacons of enlightenment,
Returning to the place where ancestors once stood.

As they dance in the wind it's hypnotic to the eye,
I'm relieved from urban anxiety I left behind so long ago,
Relaxation of the mind, memories revisited,
An atmosphere of harmony soon to be broken.

Change arrives and with it brings laughter,
Another form of serenity distorted in a mirror.
White-washed haven, complete with a garden of peace
I hope its presence will never cease.

Katherine Bridges (14)
Solihull School, Solihull

Old Git

I don't wanna be an old git
Don't wanna grow up old and cruel
Don't wanna tell my kids off
Don't wanna send them to school

I wanna be fun and keep in touch
Muck about with my kids
But I don't want to cling to youth
When my life has hit the skids

Old women who put on make-up
Old men who wear tight T-shirts
The women look older than they really do
The men look so bad it hurts

No, I don't wanna be an old git
I wanna be a fun-loving guy
Play with my kids and laugh in the sun
Be an old git? Never gonna try.

Matthew Tyler (14)
Solihull School, Solihull

Riverside Cottage

I remember Riverside Cottage,
I saw how the sun always shines,
I saw the cold, unfriendly, stone walls of the cottage,
I remember the palette of flowers draped on the vines.

I heard the crunch of shrivelled brown leaves beneath my feet,
I felt the smooth leathery leaves hanging,
I heard the snow-white lambs in the field innocently bleat,
I heard the beautiful song of the chaffinch singing.

I remember the broken rickety old gate that we always pass,
I tasted the plain, simple country air,
I tasted fresh cut grass,
I remember Riverside Cottage.

Elizabeth Ready (14)
Solihull School, Solihull

My Brother

It was the dirty clothes caked in mud
Lying neatly in a pile on the floor,

The mouldy sandwich, not nice in the first place,
But just plain disgusting now.

It was the deflated beanbag, so limp and lifeless,
Too small for him now, I think it's relieved,

The dusty mirror and hair products beside,
Never used or even looked upon with the thought of use.

It was the bed at an angle taking up most of the room,
With its covers in a pile, expecting to be made themselves,

The prized possessions out on display and frequently used,
The laptop, the guitar, the iPod, the phone.

It was all of these things combined together
Which best remind me of him.

Callum Fisher (14)
Solihull School, Solihull

Death Personified

No living soul truly understands death
They fear him, they despise him, they hide from him
A shrouded figure of screams and sadness
Upon his thrown built of blood and bone,
Riding swiftly on his devilish steed,
Bringing torture, pain and misery.
However for some this is not so
Death is kind, death is peaceful, death is rest
A welcome release from a life of torment
A bright escape from the darkness of Earth
A soul rescued from a body of pain
Encircled by light, a song of happiness
Resting forever embraced in his arms
Death is eternal, my saviour, my love.

Taimoor Rashid (14)
Solihull School, Solihull

The Zen Walk

I remember my mother and I going to Packwood House
We observed the beautiful gardens with admiration.

I saw the lichen parading in many different shades of green
Their textures ranging from brittle to woolly, like a winter coat.

I touched the old rotting wood that crumbled beneath my fingers
I felt the fibreglass, rough under my palms.

I smelt the fresh spring air, clean and unblemished
I smelt the lingering scent of humans inside the house.

I tasted a leaf, crunchy like lettuce
I tasted the leaf, it had no flavour.

Matthew Bottomley (14)
Solihull School, Solihull

Holiday In The Sun

Holiday in the sun,
There's the sea and the beach
And lots of other fun.

There's plenty of ice cream to go around.
There's the shells and the fish
That people have found.

There is a lot of sand,
But when it comes to the big sandcastles
You might need a hand.

If you are lucky you might go to the fair,
If you go on the fast ones,
You might get messy hair.

When the day has ended,
And it's time to go home.
When you get in
You will need to use a comb.

Emily Riley (11)
The Northicote School, Wolverhampton

White Desert

There is a white desert
That all think is perfect and clear
But I know different.
The landscape is covered
In deep valleys, through which,
Red rivers flow
And the ugly scars of gashed long healed.
No one knows.
But I do.
I know of the forces
That shaped the valleys
And of the regrets
As the red tears fall.
Now it is too late.
They think the worst is over
But it has only just begun.
The old ways may have died,
But new ways can be found.
They will never know,
They will think it is still clear.
They will never see
What I have done.

Lydia Dungey (15)
The Northicote School, Wolverhampton

The Wolf

T he wolf is graceful,
H e howls at the moon,
E very day he hunts for prey,

W hen he howls everyone hears,
O n the night he sleeps silently,
L oving to his family and brave too,
F inally he creeps back to his den.

Lauren Smith
The Northicote School, Wolverhampton

Welcoming To Hell

Once God's beauty,
Standing gracious and tall
Long blonde hair
Stunning them all.

But who could predict,
Who could tell,
The horrors about to face her
The welcoming to Hell?

Up from the waters he came
Seeking her beauty,
His power uncontrollable,
Against her timid bodice.

Ran, she did
To a temple well known,
Hoping for protection,
Against the god on her heels.

But the goddess she asked,
Saw nothing but disgust,
Left the beauty alone,
Scared to the bone.

The god caught her,
And took what he wished,
Then left her broken,
Whimpering, dismissed.

The goddess in disgust,
Saw right by her,
To curse this beauty,
To be forever alone.

Now, no longer a beauty,
But a monster, hidden,
She again stops every man in her tracks,
But not for the right reasons.

Her name you ask?
Oh you know it well,
But did you know the tragic story, behind this woman's tale?
Her name . . . Medusa.
The god that did this? Poseidon.
The goddess? Athena.

Louise Weaver (15)
The Northicote School, Wolverhampton

Angel In The Sky

In the clouds
Where you now lie
Little angel in the sky

Sleeping soundly
Until the day you wake
But before that day my heart will break

So I will wait
My heart full of woe
Patiently waiting for my time to go

Then in the sky
We both will be
Finally together, just you and me

Looking up
I cry and frown
Wondering why you can't come down

The realisation
Strikes my lonely heart
Knowing that we will never be apart

There's no separation
Just because you are now above
Our relationship carries on because of love.

Elizabeth Elliot
The Northicote School, Wolverhampton

The Unknown Season

A season brings the colours green, pink and blue,
See if you can figure out my poem, I'll give you a clue.
Trees are full of ongoing love,
Red blossom sways on the trees above,
Falling gracefully as they swift to the ground,
A soft fall without a sound,
The smell of fresh cut grass fills the air,
Reminiscing the melody of the glowing flare,
Towards the shore, the golden sand it shines,
Merging together as the tide collides,
Joy and happiness fills the beach,
Of those who surf and who that reach,
For the sandcastle is left, yet still to be made,
There's dancing and singing like a summer parade,
Laughs and cheers spread throughout,
Hearing the sounds of people shout,
The sun sparkles, filling the sky with light,
Glimmering shimmers, oh so bright,
There's the clues, can you figure out,
What season my poem's talking about?

Shaneaqua Edwards (13)
The Northicote School, Wolverhampton

The Darkness

The darkness is a velvety quilt, resting across the skies,
On top of towns and cities, bringing a sparkle to people's eyes.
Sprinkled with glitter (the twinkling stars),
You can see the beauty of them, even from afar.
It keeps the world snug and sound,
After dark not a thing can be found,
Wide awake not a creature, not a soul,
Not a mouse in a house, a horse or its foal.
Everybody prays before saying goodnight,
But not long after the dark turns to light!

Hayley Samuels (12)
The Northicote School, Wolverhampton

What Is Weather?

Weather can be lightning, shocking you;
It can be soft rain trickling into your shoe.
Can it be a gentle snowflake slowly dropping onto your fragile face,
Or littering hail shooting down like bullets trying to win a race?

Is weather something that appears when you look out the window
Or is it like a rock that never grows old or fades away no matter where you go?
Could it be a silent breeze
Or the hot blazing sun shining on the beautiful trees?

Will it disturb your peace,
Or will it warm you like a golden fleece?
No matter how many times the weather will show,
The truth is we will never know.

Tor Bennett Williams (11)
The Northicote School, Wolverhampton

Gone

Now that you're not here
The world seems to go on
I will forever love you
Now that you're gone

I have no one to talk to
No one to hold my hand
That when I fly my plane
I'll know I will never land

There is no one beside me
No one to say I look nice
That when I say, 'Vodka'
There is no one to say, 'Ice?'

Paige Woods (15)
The Northicote School, Wolverhampton

The Defeat Of Gods (The Fall of Scylla and Charybdis)

Follow one's gaze along the battered tide
Swelling and writhing with warfare of pride
The rise of the great gods, as the weak fall
The rise of grand Scylla and Charybdis.

Shaken earth bears witness to the portent
Desolation. Dry, the decision rent
The deities' destruction almighty
Does one ever see such power, prithee?

Small, insignificant seed, plots its course
Honourable warriors at the helm
Navigates the hostile waters between
Unseen.

Sam Bentham (15)
The Northicote School, Wolverhampton

Vampires

They are creatures of darkness.
Their soul is lost.
They are immortal,
But what is the cost?

Their humanity has gone
In its place is despair.
They're surrounded by a sea of sadness,
But do they really care?

They come from horror stories.
They are monsters of the night.
This animal will infect you,
So beware of the bite.

Charlotte Skidmore (14)
The Northicote School, Wolverhampton

The Pain Of A Weapon

This can lead to death,
With a point going into your body.
Red blood dripping.
There's too many weapons,
But this hurts the most.
You imagine . . .
A blade punching one of your organs
It's like getting hit by a car at 60 miles per hour,
This must stop or . . .
More people will drop.

Luke Chagger (12)
The Northicote School, Wolverhampton

Fashion

F ashion is the new passion
A ll the products cost some money
S o in my words this is not funny
H appily fashion overcomes my life
I n this life it includes a man to moan about his wife
O n the fact that she wears too much make-up
N o one can stop me at the opportunity of fashion.

Megan Gallagher
The Northicote School, Wolverhampton

The Life Of A Tiger

Tigers are bright in every way
But they pay in another way
With one blow to the head
The tiger drops down dead
With an ending like this
What is the life of a tiger?

Amy Evans (12)
The Northicote School, Wolverhampton

Wounded

She looks, but she never sees
She hears, but she never believes
She touches, but she never feels
She's wounded and she never heals.

Samantha Nightingale (15)
The Northicote School, Wolverhampton

Three Words Can Save A Life

In the dark winter, I walk through the snow
I wonder, I ponder, is he thinking about me?
Wandering listlessly to and fro, through the dark woods,
Slowly freezing, *crunch, crunch, crunch*
I start to run, I daren't look round
My heartbeat pounding louder and louder in my ear,
Drowning out the sounds of the *crunch, crunch, crunch* from behind me,
I see a sign for a closed bridge,
I slow down when I come to the end of the bridge,
I climb up on the unfinished railings; I look down to see the reflection of the moonlight and the bridge in the shimmering water,
I think to myself, *it will soon be over, just jump and you could be so much happier.*

I . . .

I feel someone grab my hand from behind me, the footsteps and my heartbeat have stopped.
He pulls me from the unfinished rafters and railings, he pulls me close to him, and he only whispers three words,
Those three words saved my life.

Those words are . . .

I love you.

I remember so clearly that night, that someone would follow me through the coldest of nights, and only want to say those words.

Rhiannon Thorpe (16)
The Orchard Centre (PRU), Wolverhampton

My Animal Family

In my house . . .

I have a bull, a strong and strict bull.
He always orders people around and tells people what he thinks.
I always pester him for things and he says, 'Don't you think you have enough?'
I call him Dad.

I have a peacock, a colourful and beautiful peacock.
She is very supporting and she will do anything for me.
She is friendly, loving and caring towards her family.
I call her Mom.

I have a ferret, an annoying, lively ferret
He always sulks if he doesn't get his own way.
He expects people to do everything for him.
Despite all that, I love him.
I call him Brother.

I have a cat, a cute cat.
She always jumps out and scares you to death.
One minute she is over the other side of the room
And the next she is on my lap.
She is always up to mischief and I get the blame for it
But people always say she loves me really.
I call her Sister.

Then there's me, the cheetah.
Always protecting people and caring for my family.
I would do anything for them because they mean the world to me.

Lewis Turton (14)
The Orchard Centre (PRU), Wolverhampton

I Lose Myself

The arguments have started again,
They're loud and they scare me.
I learnt long ago not to scream,
Not to get involved,
Just to lose myself.

I lock the door, I turn on my music,
Now I start to lose myself.
I lose myself in the music,
I lose myself in the anger,
I lose myself in the pain.

The shouting is louder now,
And I can even hear banging.
Block it out, just block it out . . .
I have to lose myself.

Chair in front of the door, music turned up,
I lose myself in the music,
I lose myself in the depression,
I lose myself in the razor blades.

These are just memories though,
The arguments . . . the fights, they're gone now.
My scars are healed and I'm happy.
But one thing that will never leave me,
Is the tendency I have to lose myself.

Julia Scheyer (14)
The Orchard Centre (PRU), Wolverhampton

The World As We Know It

I wake up in the morning, get up, get dressed,
Brush my teeth, wash my face, start feeling stressed.

The buzzing box in the corner of the room,
Tales of malicious militia and of new regime resume.
How long until those poetic promises that won them their prize
Become nothing but simply lazy lies?

On the way, a battered bum,
Nothing but his badly-spelt sign and assortment of rum.
Gaudy graffiti scratched into a park bench,
I finally arrive with my fingers clenched.

My words whoosh over a million peers' heads,
And so it's times like these that little me dreads.
Nervous of looks, of make-up and hearing them hiss.
Bugging my mates with, 'Does my bum look big in this?'

Do we really know how good we have it?
Is the world awry or am I just being an idiot?
In slums so squalid the rats turn away,
Do their lives improve the more we pray?

Surely there must be those who care,
Those who abhor the world's despair?
Is anyone trying to halt humanity's crime?
Maybe now and maybe never, but perhaps in good time.

Mariah Antill (15)
The Orchard Centre (PRU), Wolverhampton

Evacuee

Today I left my parents
So now I'm sad and glum
I really miss my dad
Even my nagging mum

I now live in the country
On a smelly farm
I live with two old people
Who fill me with alarm

I have no clothes
I have no toys
And surrounded by
Many nasty boys

I hate all the animals
And all the country air
I want to go home
I'll be happy when I get there

The war is finally over
I'm so smiley and glad
I want to go and see my family
And stop feeling so bad.

Victoria Louise Shaw (13)
The Orchard Centre (PRU), Wolverhampton

Being A Gay Teenager

Living in a world where I can't be myself
Can't come out in fear of getting kicked down
Living in a world where I don't have rights
I can't live my life
Watch what I say, could slip up and say I am gay
All the time hoping
I won't be found out.

Rebecca Goodhead (14)
The Orchard Centre (PRU), Wolverhampton

Rocky Ride

Time to ride
The rocky ride
Twist and turn
Up and down
Side to side
I feel sick
Now
Here comes the
Loop-the-loop
Scream and shout
That's what it's
All about
Now
Comes the drop
Up we go
Scream and shout
Down we dive
Are we still
Alive?
Arrgghh!

Joe Goldsmith (12)
The Orchard Centre (PRU), Wolverhampton

Sometimes The Lion

Sometimes
The lion
Runs to catch his prey.
Like a speeding motorbike.
Escaping from the police.

Sometimes
The lion
Swallows her food
Like a snake eating
Its prey whole.

Edward Shore (12)
The Orchard Centre (PRU), Wolverhampton

My Life

This is my life and I am not lying
My dad is sick and he is dying.
My nephew wasn't very well
He was fifteen weeks early and he went through hell.
My nephew also had an operation when he was two on his head
He made a recovering by staying in bed.

My life at school is good
I don't have to walk around wearing a hood.
I don't get bullied at school
I think it's real cool.
I have lots of good mates
When we meet up I have to remember the dates.

I made some friends in my new street
We always go out and meet.
I like to play on computer games
But sometimes I don't remember the names.
Well that's the end of my rhyme
Also I don't have the time.

Jordan Lloyd (13)
The Orchard Centre (PRU), Wolverhampton

Evacuee

Today I have been taken away to a place I don't know.
Where am I going?
What do I do?
There is a big man standing next to me taking me on a train.
I hear a whistling noise
What can that be?
Now there is a big metal thing with steam coming out.
He has taken me to his house, it is in the country.
When will the war be over?
I want to go home
I might run away . . .

Chelsea Williams (13)
The Orchard Centre (PRU), Wolverhampton

Elements

Elements are sometimes helpful and sometimes deadly
But they also help to show you
How to avoid the consequences.

Fire is blazing, raging and dangerous
So beware of the cinders
But it's nice to have a fire on a cold winter day.

Water is cool, calm, refreshing and can extinguish fire
But even something friendly has a dark side
As the sea is friendly when it is calm,
But when a storm comes the sea turns violent.

Air is sometimes more harmless than the other elements but looks don't change it.
Sometimes the air can be someone's last thing they see as the air can become a hurricane.

Earth is one of the most dangerous elements as it can be an earthquake that can crack the planet in two
But can help you out of tight spots sometimes.

Callum Derek Andrews (14)
The Orchard Centre (PRU), Wolverhampton

Alive In War

The war came
I had to leave my family
I was sad and upset
I was angry with Hitler
What's the whole point?

All that's going through my mind
Are my mom and dad
Thinking what they are doing,
Are they alive, dead or what?
I wonder where they are.

I have been forced to live
With an old grumpy man
I hate being here
I cannot return
Home until this stupid war is over
I hope it won't be long
I want my mom and dad.

Glyn Anthony Cieron Smith (13)
The Orchard Centre (PRU), Wolverhampton

My Best Cousin, Kirsty

My best cousin Kirsty
She is the best, she looks after me,
When people call me nasty names.
She always warns me to be careful
She always helps me with my writing
She makes me laugh when I'm upset.
She plays with me at football and dancing and singing.
She tells the bullies to leave me alone because I have problems.
She always sits by me so I'm not lonely.
I go to her house and go on her laptop
Which has a background of puppies
She has a necklace saying 'Best Cousin'
And she is.

Seranne Behenna (13)
The Orchard Centre (PRU), Wolverhampton

Life As A Teenager

Seven years I am stuck like this
Seven years stuck in this deep, dark hole of depression
Seven years with no way to get out
Seven years of having my tears smudge my suicide note
Seven years of telling people we are not all the same
Seven years of sweet razor wounds
Seven years of pointless bleeding
Seven years of going through the changes alone
Seven years of needing to be wanted
Seven years of never being heard
Seven years of stereotypical views
Seven years of never telling anyone
Seven years of hell
This is a teenager's life, this is my life.

Beth Nangle (14)
The Orchard Centre (PRU), Wolverhampton

Open Arms

It's good to have that special friend
Have them till the never end
They stick by you
You stick by them
Without them you'd be lost
They're the one you love the most
When they are there you don't feel blue
That is because they stand by you
Everyone has their open arms
Or a hand for you to hold
When you're feeling down or cold
So just remember, never let them go
As one day they might be gone
And then you'll be all alone.

Jasmine Ross (14)
The Orchard Centre (PRU), Wolverhampton

Friends

I think my friends are amazing.
I love them the entire highest amount possible.
I would risk my own life or die for them.
They make coming to the Centre worthwhile.
I think they are some of the most amazing people ever to be alive.
If I didn't have them I wouldn't be anything.
They are a massive part of my life.
I never want to lose them.
They are incredibly special.
They are always there for me.
They are trustworthy.
They are gems.
I try and be the best friend to them as I can be.

Cameron Nock (15)
The Orchard Centre (PRU), Wolverhampton

Friends

Remembering the day that we first met, out on the playground
When you just said those few words that felt like the beginning of forever.
'Will you be my friend?'
Over the years we never grew apart as others came, went and left our hearts.
We always have something to talk about even though we know each other inside out.
We went through the childish fights and battled through it all,
You know you're always going to have a helping hand if you trip and fall.
And you know if you need an opinion you can always come to me,
And even if we don't agree about the same things you won't lose a friend in me.
What I'm trying to say is that you've never left my heart and we'll battle through it all and we'll
Never be apart.

Shannon Jones & Megan Lockwood (14)
Wickersley School & Sports College, Wickersley

Soldier of WWI

Uniforms ripped and scuffed but with pride they are worn
Lungs choked in dust, feet blistered and torn.

Soldiers down as dead as flies,
Others up and fighting for their lives.

Many miles we have trodden in this godforsaken land and heat hot as hell
And the horrors that we witness, our loved ones we don't tell

Caught and captured, some shoved against a wall,
We do our duty with pride and pray that we won't fall.

The Germans have their place here in the fight
We hope in years yet to come they're not our nightmares in the night.

But we have our duty to do today, our orders have come through;
It's yet another compound to be cleared by me and you.

So roll on the end of tour when from Hell we can depart
And a few months home with loved ones that we cannot wait to start.

We stand and fight with all our heart,
Holding our guns till death us do part.

Fighting for our country; we do best
Trying to be better than all the rest.

The World War I soldiers; where are they now? Sat at home tall and proud
Or did some of them fall to the ground . . . ?

Wives at home cry out loud,
Thinking of the husband that did them proud.

News is spread far and wide,
That another loved one/friend has sadly died,

But the past is far and the future is near,
No need to run scared in fear.

Ben Higgins (14)
Wickersley School & Sports College, Wickersley

Love Amongst Hate

Evil, stone-cold hearts
showing scenes of
revenge one second
by second . . .

Simple, it was,
for them to kill
without depression
any emotions

Drifting sand
sense of blood
gun on hands,
bodies on ground

Autumn past
war still lasts
soldiers waiting,
waiting for the light

To come back
while branches of
trees are falling
- falling to meet their leaves

Spring is now reaching
children are counting,
counting for the day
he returns

A distance away
He sees a wave
running through the
tall grass and dandelions

They finally meet together,
but thinking back to the
lives that were lost
guilt is only left behind

The sweetness of the tea
and tenderness of love;
from his children
melts the unforgettable
guiltiness inside.

Shirley Ngan (12)
Wickersley School & Sports College, Wickersley

Wolves

As the moon came out and became a new moon.
Creeping and crawling out from the den of broken trees,
The ghastly and grim wolves came out to play.
As little girls' shattered broken dreams,
Because the wolves had found their prey.

As the alpha's eyes flared a deep red, the other wolves knew it was teatime.
An old deer was tonight's sorry victim, so they headed home carrying the fine meaty meal.
The family were all waiting to share their tales of the day,
The pups yelped with glee, when they saw the feast arriving.
Their father the hero.

As the flames roared and soared, the people ran in terror.
A simple forest fire had now spread across the board.
The screams could be heard miles away, as human roast was burning like hay.
The stench clung to your nose, the smell of burning wood, skin and memories.
As families screamed for loved lost ones.

But over the other side of the world, people were enjoying the fire,
Because on a cold summer's night it's your heart's only desire.
You may thank God that even the most evil of people can show love
Or you may curse God because even the most loving of people can still be evil.

Molly Burtoft (13)
Wickersley School & Sports College, Wickersley

The Cobra

In the mask of the night,
Now the bats have started flight,
Hidden in the undergrowth,
Is something horrid, something gross.

Sliding gently out of its cover,
Followed closely by its brother,
And mother,
And lover.

Eyes set firmly on its prey,
Waiting for the break of day.
As the sun raises to the sky,
The small fieldmouse is going to die.

Isn't it peculiar how a cobra, of all creatures,
Can love and share with all of its friends?
This is one of its many features,
That confuses me.

Past the cobra walks a human,
Trying to find some food for his pan,
Gently grasping his long, thin gun,
It's a call of nature, not just for fun.

In the blink of an eye a deer is shot,
Ready and waiting for its long sleep in a pot,
The man mourns the death of the innocent animal,
Many would class the man as a criminal,
However he has mouths to feed.

It is weird and strange,
How something so deranged,
Can love and care,
And give a share.

Joe Oxspring (12)
Wickersley School & Sports College, Wickersley

Well There's This School . . .

Well there's this school,
It thinks it's cool.
It sends us on trips,
But it's such a fix.
£500 just for one day,
I could buy a new car or have a holiday!

They rip us off with expensive food,
And the dinner ladies are just plain rude.
Shouting at us, telling us to go outside,
So we just run off to go and hide.

Why do teachers act like they care?
Detentions, sanctions, it's just not fair.
What's with the respect we have to give,
And what's with them telling us how to live?

Bottle-green jumpers, are you serious?
Ties and top buttons, you're sending us delirious.
We're all individuals but we look the same,
We all think this uniform is just so lame.

Nagging at us to get a good grade,
Once we have it we'll start to fade.
GCSEs? We're just fourteen,
Let's be honest, we're not that keen.

I thought education was just for us!

Jemma Poole, Devon Round (14) & Nicole Turtle (13)
Wickersley School & Sports College, Wickersley

Soldiers Of War

We are the warrior of life and death
We are the superiority of war at its best
We are the fighters for peace not war
We fight from our hearts down to the core
We fight freedom, law and order
We are the US marines
Live with it.

Those who stand in their path are cut down,
Slaughtered in their own hometown
They live in terror, fear and fright
Their enemy travels throughout their land, night after night after night
They are the civilians
And they live with it.

I am their ranks
Their ranks of evil and tanks
I fight for money not glory
So my life's not much of a story
Those who stand in my way,
Will be shot, they're not here to stay
We are militia
And I can live with it.

Matthew Boyce-Boardman (14) & Oliver King (13)
Wickersley School & Sports College, Wickersley

Music Harmony

Feel the beat under your feet
Let your heart go, go, go
Listen to the drums go boom, boom
Listen to the rhythm
Hear the guitar go crazy
Play your keyboard like a madman
Feel the beat, oh yeah
Sing your heart out, yeah, yeah, yeah, boom!

Anya Gill (12)
Wickersley School & Sports College, Wickersley

The New Teenage Craze!

The teachers never listen
I always get the blame
They never seem to believe me
I think it's really lame

Well there I go again
Shouting out the odds
I just can't help myself
Like I'm gonna turn to God.

There's no one to talk to
And no one who cares
My mum and dad just yell
Then send me up the stairs.

I have no friends to look out for
Everyone thinks I'm mean
I cannot understand why
I'm just a normal teen

But if someone would only listen
I might just change my ways
Think before I speak
Maybe set a new teenage craze.

Emilia Shillito (11)
Wickersley School & Sports College, Wickersley

Goodbye

My rose heart has turned to thorns
My feelings for you are as cold as stone
You will howl when morning dawn
You will look for me as you roam

But I am gone, now I say goodbye
Yes my eyes do fill with tears
But though I cry
Does not mean I will forget the years

The happy and glee times
The sad and scary
But we must climb
And be wary

These were the days
And now they're done
I will love you always
But I must run

So I leave you this note
Because I could not bear
This is my antidote
Just promise me something, you will take care.

Jemma Daisy Heathcoate (12)
Wickersley School & Sports College, Wickersley

Love Amongst Hate

As soon as red eyes, are laid upon,
Glowing clear, luminous like the sun,
My heart is set, and forevermore,
Shall not be broken, against the law,

Law of which, pulls us apart,
To keep the secret, for a start,
Sworn to secrecy, I must never tell,
Any living soul about this hell,

The urge to bite, and constant thirst,
Why am I, so painfully cursed?
A fragile human, I long to be,
But when I hunt it takes over me,

Words can't describe, our love so strong,
A girl like this, I have waited so long,
Humans shatter like glass, in compared,
Rather glass, than her heart teared,

Because when the vampire, comes out to play,
Irresponsible for my actions, lead to dismay
She deserves, so much better than me,
And so it is forevermore.

Lauren Wainwright (13)
Wickersley School & Sports College, Wickersley

Back In My Days

BIMD if we wanted to talk we couldn't just drop them a call,
BIMD we couldn't just go and spend 100 quid in a mall,
BIMD I'd walk down the street and people would know my name,
BIMD if we did something wrong we would have to take the blame,
BIMD we couldn't walk in and just turn the light on,
BIMD we'd get the cane if we blamed it on anyone,
BIMD if we wanted some veg we could just walk out to the yard,
BIMD if we wore a hoodie people would think we were hard.

Although we weren't all classed as equal,
We weren't put into stereotypes,
We knew how to make our own fun,
Without the use of alcohol or drugs,
But many people prefer the modern day of living,
But sometimes it's nice to see a bit of giving.

BIMD we wouldn't care what people thought,
BIMD we used the manners we were taught.

BIMD things were different.

Alana Jackson & Chanelle Clarke (13)
Wickersley School & Sports College, Wickersley

War Never Changes

War is a battle of pride,
Duty calls for every soldier.
There can only be one winner,
History is written by the victor,
But history is never written as
War always finds a place to rest its head.
Grenades fly around like birds,
Blood pumps around the body as fast as a bullet
No matter who has the biggest guns,
It's who is handling them is the real question.
History can never be written as war rages.
And war . . . war never changes!

Christian Hague (12)
Wickersley School & Sports College, Wickersley

Remember When You'd Say . . .

Remember when you'd say we'd always be best mates;
But that would soon change when we had our first date.
My heart started beating, I couldn't sit still.
You asked me what's wrong, I said nothing until.
You took me by the hand and led me to your heart,
I remember us thinking what a beautiful start.
By the end of the night, I started to think;
Is this true love or is it just a link?

Remember when you'd say I was the only girl for you;
But that was just a lie, none of it was true.
Should have known by the glances you gave;
The way you'd smiled, the way you'd behave.
You left me for her, my life is now a blur;
Stop pretending you give a damn;
Our relationship was just a sham.

You've made a hole, but you can't break my soul!

Georgina Gunn, Hollie Sheppard & Courtney Sutton (14)
Wickersley School & Sports College, Wickersley

Love And Hate

I love my family, they are so close to me.
I love my fashion and my denim jeans.
I love the beach, collecting pebbles and shells.
I love the glorious sound of the soft chiming bells.
I love my friends, we love setting trends.
I love my mobile and clothes, when will this younger generation end?
I hate all the stupid crime and drugs.
I hate all the violence, where is the love?
I hate all the guns and the weapons we have, where are the giggles and barrels of laughs?
I hate how readings get shoved out of the way, it's time for creativity to take over and stay.
I hate all the litter and smoking too, it's time to make a difference for me and you.

Lauren Carr (11)
Wickersley School & Sports College, Wickersley

I Just Don't

I don't like to curl and toss my hair,
I don't cross my legs when I sit on a chair.
I don't wear long nails or put in extensions,
I don't want to grow up and marry a Frenchman.

I don't go around wearing a fake smile.
I don't like to sharpen my nails with a file.
I don't like to pose and smirk in a mirror,
I don't wear dresses at nightclubs that shimmer.

I don't always look the best,
But it's guaranteed I will stand out from all the rest.
Being me I'm not like all the others,
I would much rather stay at home and play with my brothers.

I know I am weird,
But that's just me.
Be my friend, and you'll soon see!

Nicole Cooper & Eleanor Dovey (12)
Wickersley School & Sports College, Wickersley

Do They Care?

Do they feel guilty?
It seems not.
Do they mean it when they say you can rot?
Maybe they do.
Have they ever been treated the same?
Maybe it's just their own sick game.

Will it carry on for many more days?
Maybe they'll see the error of their ways.
Do they like it when they see you cry?
Maybe, if their hearts are dry.

Do they lie awake in bed?
Maybe they can't wait to see you dead.

Sophie Gibson (13)
Wickersley School & Sports College, Wickersley

Love

Love is like paper,
It can tear easily,
But if you look after it,
It will last.

I will love you forever,
And then in Heaven
I devour your love,
And keep it in my heart,
For your love keeps me alive.

My love for you is stronger than an ox,
I love you and always will,
I hope you do too,
You lighten my day,
It's boring without you,
Baby I love you!

Chloe Wilkinson (12)
Wickersley School & Sports College, Wickersley

The Hordes

They all smell like skin and rust
To them your body is a must
Their lust for you just cannot wait,
Your skin, it tastes like choc-o-late.
All the crows just sit there waiting
Perched on top of the battered slating
Wondering what I'm going to eat
Whilst I am so upbeat
I only see you on the floor
And your heart's not beating anymore
There's an iron smell of blood in the air
As you fall into Hell's snare.
Sadness, happiness, anger, fear, anxiousness, pity.
All feelings are absent
In this undead city.

Owen King (12)
Wickersley School & Sports College, Wickersley

Maybe If . . .

Maybe, if lessons were more fun we'd listen
Maybe, if they started with quizzes we'd pay attention
Maybe, if the teachers could have a laugh we'd like them
Maybe, if we did all this more people would attend school
Maybe, if we'd stop bullying, people would like school
Maybe, if dinner time was more fun people would actually leave their seats.

M adness
A nger
Y obs
B ullies
E ducation

I diots
F ails.

Zak Anthony Bailey (13)
Wickersley School & Sports College, Wickersley

The Life Train

Life is a train, a fast, fast train,
You have little to lose and lots to gain.
You choose the right or you choose the wrong,
You have lots of time cos the journey's long.
You go to school to learn the right,
Because life is a beautiful sight.
If you choose the wrong it will be bad,
Drugs and cigarettes, it's very, very sad.
Choose the way that you think,
Or in your life you will just sink.
Then your train goes round a bend,
Now the journey's come to an end.

Abigail Adams & Hannah Horton (12)
Wickersley School & Sports College, Wickersley

What A Friend Is

A friend is someone we turn to, when our spirits lift above.
A friend is someone we treasure, for our friendship is a gift.
A friend is someone who fills our lives with beauty, joy and care.
And makes the whole world we live in a better, happier prayer.
A friend is warm and precious like gold,
A friendship will never become old, and they will always be there in health and in death.
A friend always helps you when you're weak, makes you laugh when you're down.
But most of all they never let you feel like you've been pushed around!

Meghan Webb (12)
Wickersley School & Sports College, Wickersley

What's Next?

We have a family; they don't,
We have a mobile; they don't,
We have food to eat; they don't,
We have games; they don't,
We have education; they don't,
We have a home; they don't,
We have books; they don't,
We have a bed; they don't,
We have fresh water; they don't,
We have TVs; they don't,
What's next?

Oliver Blake & Alex Stronach (12)
Wickersley School & Sports College, Wickersley

Dolphin Poem

Swimming through the waves at super light speed.
Caught in the nets, the boats make them bleed.
If they could they'd swim away.
But that will come another day.
On the boat the songs they sing.
Dolphins laugh while the nets they sling.
But still one dolphin always on the look
Just in case in the nets a dolphin gets stuck.
Eco the warrior, guardian of the sea.
Swimming along to the sweet melody.

Michael Taylor (11)
Wickersley School & Sports College, Wickersley

The Sun

The sun shines down on me
As I jump with glee.
I look up to the clear sky
I get a whiff of apple pie
It is a smell so sweet
It would go well in this scorching heat
As I bought some ice cream
Took a lick, it was as hot as a sunbeam
I sat under the tree for shade
And watched the colourful parade.

Aisha Mahmood (11)
Wickersley School & Sports College, Wickersley

The Desert

The desert's scorching heat,
burning my very soul.
The barren wasteland,
with no clear end . . .
The scorpions,
burrowing under the sand,
waiting for their next victim.
Water, water, I need water.
Mirages, illusions.
The Devil is at work,
Torturing me till my last breath.

The sand burning my feet under the sun,
Each grain feels like glass,
Slicing through my skin.
The sun, forever blinding me,
Confusing me with its rays.
The wind whipping the glass-like sand in my face.
Cutting deep gashes in my skin.
Water, water, I need water.
Mirages, illusions.
The Devil is at work,
waiting for my very soul.

My time is nearly up,
Yet, still I go on,
Defying the fiend that craves my soul.
Yet all of a sudden I see civilisation,
I head towards it with my dying breath.
Finally, at last I have escaped his wrath,
Though it nearly took my life.
I am proud to have beaten the fallen one.

Luke Parkes (15)
William Bradford Community College, Earl Shilton

World Cup Glory

It's the last minute for me;
Everybody staring I see,
We're now in stoppage time,
3 minutes, I knew it would be.

This is my time,
To make the sky shine
To make the world mine;
To penetrate the net
With passion and force
The crowd cheering my name
Whaoooo! Whaoooo!

A long through ball
Use everything I've got
It's time to be me, not everything I'm not.
I take on the keeper and I'm left on the floor to rot.
The ref blows his whistle and points to the spot,
From the 4th tier I look like a dot.

Try to calm down, to have no fear
'Cause the county needs me . . .
The ball's put on the spot . . .
Trying to not look up 'cause the keeper's a cheater
Because this memory could be a keeper
I take a run-up
And strike it with passion
It was all a blur
All I could see was three lions
And also 2 stars instead of 1
After the game I could honestly say
I brought the world home.

Ryan Oswald (14)
William Bradford Community College, Earl Shilton

Dream

As I fall asleep
My dream begins . . .

Lying quietly, lying still,
eyes flickering, lips quivering,
breathing in and out.

Pictures drifting in my head,
Floating
like feathers,
And anything can happen.

Thoughts circling and spiralling
as I fall into a
deep sleep.

Times gone by
are
distant memories

Pictures drifting in my head,
Floating
like feathers,
and anything can happen.

There always seems to be
A part that is missing,
And the dream
F a d e s into
Reality.

Elysia Newton (14)
William Bradford Community College, Earl Shilton

What Have I Done?

I feel so isolated
It's not fair
They don't actually care
But what have I done?

They are always picking on me
'specially the boy, Lee
He pulls my hair,
Thumps and kicks me
But what have I done?

I always try to hide
Keep out of their way
They say I'm always going to pay
But what have I done?

I'm always on my own
I try not to moan
I'm covered in bruises
They say I'm a loser
But what have I done?

My dad tells me to stand up for myself
I think that's what I just might do
Here they come now
I get ready, I clench my fist . . .

Jasmin Copson (15)
William Bradford Community College, Earl Shilton

Life

Life is too precious to care about stupid stuff,
So go have fun, party and fall in love!
Say what you want to say
Do what you want to do
Regret nothing.
And don't let the people who don't matter,
Bring you down.

Chelsea King (15)
William Bradford Community College, Earl Shilton

New Year, New Change

People seem to think
The world is an angry place,
Full of wars, aggression and hatred
Disagreements and arguments.
But from as far as I can see
When the clock strikes midnight,
On December 31st,
And the dawn of a new year arrives.
There is love.
Love all around the world
A time for change,
To turn over a new leaf.
A fresh beginning.
Hatred is forgotten,
Replaced by those special in your life.

As far as I can see,
That's all that matters.
But why
Carry this on?
24/7
365 days a year
Until the following December 31st
When the clock chimes midnight.

Amy Armitage (15)
William Bradford Community College, Earl Shilton

The World Cup

Today is the day, the final game.
The tension is high.
The opposition are ashamed
As a shot by Crouch hits the net.
The whole crowd roars.
We have won it again!

Conor Salmon (14)
William Bradford Community College, Earl Shilton

Time

Time is like a creeping snail
Tick-tock, tick-tock
I feel like I'm in jail
Chained up by the clock
By the ticking clock
All I can see is the lock
Every minute is going slow
The clock is hanging low
Wishing five minutes have gone
Why is this day so long?

Tick-tock, tick-tock
I wish time could go
I wish it was not so slow
Time ticking every second
Hearing that ticking noise
Always wishing minutes could go faster
Tick-tock, tick-tock
Why is time so slow?
Time moves like a snail
Time never goes fast
Time is slow
Tick-tock, tick-tock!

Ben Glew (14)
William Bradford Community College, Earl Shilton

You And I

My eyes brighten up and dance
Around like stars when your presence is near.
My heart misses a beat when you are close by my side.
The world will stop just for me to show my affection to you.
Then my face meets with yours . . . we start to kiss.
I fall down and gaze at your stunning eyes
And as I breathe my last breath just for you.

I die with you!

Jonnie Skinner (14)
William Bradford Community College, Earl Shilton

Inside

They came for him today
                He was very lost
                              They took him away
                To the inside

They found it very sad
                They didn't understand
                              They understand he's bad
                On the inside

I was there one day
                Waiting for them to arrive
                              Like they always do
                On the inside

She was very sad that day
                The day that it happened
                              I thought she'd get away
                From the inside

If it never happened
                It would be quite nice
                              But I will always hate it
                On the inside.

Lewis Wright (15)
William Bradford Community College, Earl Shilton

To My Love

Your heart is my home,
Full of joy and love,
Your eyes are like stars,
Glistening in the dark,
Your hugs are like forever,
Warming me up,
Your hand clutching tight,
As we walk side by side,
Whispering, 'I love you so much . . .'

Eve Elizabeth Moth (15)
William Bradford Community College, Earl Shilton

All Alone In This World

Every day I would walk,
Having nobody for me to talk.
Sitting in the corners all alone,
Fiddling with my mobile phone.

Seeing all the people walking by,
None of them stop to say hi.
Most of the time I give a sigh,
Then later on I want to cry.

There was one person I wanted.
My chances of seeing her were haunted.
I am here and she is there,
My chances of seeing her again are rare.

The days go on and on,
And all the tears from my eyes are gone.
The weekend comes and I am free,
And my world lightens with happiness, and glee.

I am all alone in this world,
All the bullies against me hurl.
I want to be a different man.
Anything I need to do, I can.

Keiran Gibbs (15)
William Bradford Community College, Earl Shilton

Why Me?

Bang! Bang! Bang!
There was a knock on the door
The enemy was here
The one I had been waiting for

He stabbed me
With his big cold eyes
Peering down at me
That one I despise

His hand flew
Into my belly
My head split
My legs were jelly

Why me?
The one you want
Why me?
The one you're after.

Katie Short (14)
William Bradford Community College, Earl Shilton

Untitled

I don't know how to feel
You say you love me
But then you turn and leave
It's like you just don't care
Like you want to hurt me
But then you return
Arms wide open
Feeding me excuses
Should I believe them?
Are they true?
Are you playing me along?
Am I worthless to you?

Bethany Keenan (15)
William Bradford Community College, Earl Shilton

Poem

The blank page stared at me,
Nothing came,
All my focus and still no idea,
What to write?
A poem of some sort . . .
What should it be based on?
My interests?
Nothing, nothing happened.
I was not inspired.
And now,
A poem, I'm writing a poem.

Shannon Hewitt (15)
William Bradford Community College, Earl Shilton

Goodbye

As you say my name
I feel my body freeze,
As my heartbeat races uncontrollably,
I listen carefully,
As your words cut through me,
Like a razor blade.
Then you turn and walk away,
I feel the sting of my tears,
As they slowly run deep inside my cuts.

Kellie-Anne Pakes (15)
William Bradford Community College, Earl Shilton

My Love

I love you
I dream about you
You brighten up my day
Without you I would be nothing
I couldn't live without you
You are my life.

Who are you?
The reason for my existence?

. . . Cheese!

Faye Whittley (15)
William Bradford Community College, Earl Shilton

Nike

From chavs to sport personality,
From red to yellow to blue.
From tracksuit to football boots,
From Wilkinson to Flintoff to Yakubu.

Helping out with different sports,
Upgrading the clothes every single day.
The Queen would be proud to wear it,
Assisting the way you play.
'Just Do It!'

Stephen Orton & Zack Taylor (15)
William Bradford Community College, Earl Shilton

Race Day

Pole position, I've just got to bring it home
The lights go red, red, red then green,
The roar of 25 bikes deafen the screams,
The crowd go wild; first corner is coming up,
Brake, downshift, downshift, then lean in
Three bikes pass round the inside.

Fourth place, need to win,
Full throttle, body tucked in,
Can't catch up, it's all gone wrong,
Coming down the straight it feels so long,
Please bike don't let go, or let the cans blow,
Lean in again my engine, it's going to blow,
Oil all over the track, this is my final hour
The last corner, I over power,
High end the bike, my race is over,
The cup is no longer in my reach.

Matthew Ceeney (14)
William Bradford Community College, Earl Shilton

Past Poets - Future Voices The Midlands & South Yorkshire

Young Writers Information

We hope you have enjoyed reading this book - and that you will continue to enjoy it in the coming years.

If you like reading and writing poetry drop us a line, or give us a call, and we'll send you a free information pack.

Alternatively if you would like to order further copies of this book or any of our other titles, then please give us a call or log onto our website at www.youngwriters.co.uk.

Young Writers Information
Remus House
Coltsfoot Drive
Peterborough
PE2 9JX
(01733) 890066